ELINOR FRY

A LEGACY OF DANCE IN

RICHMOND

PAUL N. HERBERT

Charleston H London

THE
History
PRESS

Published by The History Press
Charleston, SC 29403
www.historypress.net

First published 2013

Manufactured in the United States

ISBN 978.1.62619.146.4

Library of Congress CIP data applied for.

To Bettie Terrell Dorsey Hobson and all Miss Fry's former pupils. Long may they dance.

CONTENTS

Acknowledgements   7
Prologue   9

I. OUR MISS FRY   11
   Students Who Stayed in Dance   16
   Peter Meriwether Fry   21

II. LEARNING AND TEACHING   23
   Miss Ella Binford's Star Pupil   23
   Miss Traylor, Miss Boyer: Tray-Boy Studio   24
   The Studio at 2600 Monument Avenue   28
   Other Richmond Dance Studios   33
   Dance Ideas from Foreign Travel   35
   Mabel Puterbaugh   42
   New York City   43

III. SETTING THE STAGE   48
   Costumes   51
   Prices and Programs   55
   Some Anecdotes   58
   Very Busy Times   64
   Comings and Goings   68
   Annual Christmas Party   69

Contents

IV. Dance Themes   72

Topical and Fads   75

Gypsies, Sports, Perfumes and Cards   78

Polkas, Boogies, Waltzes and Miss Americas   79

Moon, Planets, Stars and Galaxy   81

Colonial Minuets and Dress Balls   83

Tobacco, Parades, Drill and Military   87

V. Frylics   93

Edith Lindeman Reviews   101

VI. Moments to Remember   103

"Mr. Fry"   103

Miss Fry Retires   105

Epilogue   113

Timeline   115

Notes   131

Sources   137

Index   139

About the Author   143

ACKNOWLEDGEMENTS

I'm grateful to the Valentine Richmond History Center for its research library and for allowing me to use photographs from its collection. Thank you to the Reno County Museum in Hutchinson, Kansas; Washington and Lee University; Mabel Toney of the Hollywood Cemetery for looking up cemetery records; and Sarah Herguner and Kendall Neely of St. Catherine's School. Special thanks to Banks Smither and Jaime Muehl of The History Press for their help in getting this from a Word document on my computer to the final product. Hello to my niece Kelli Ballard. Perhaps seeing her name in a book will get her interested in dancing. Or writing. Thank you to my wife, Pam; sons, Alex and Bill; and my mom and dad for being who they are and always being there. I greatly appreciate the information and assistance provided by many of Miss Fry's former pupils. Several of them scanned photographs and/or lent me photographs to scan. Thank you to Patsy Bickerstaff for editing the draft, but any and all errors are my responsibility. Most of all, thank you to Bettie Terrell Dorsey Hobson (Mrs. Hobson) for sharing her scrapbooks, for her friendship and for loading me up with cookies and other goodies during the research. Many former students told me that Miss Fry's kindness lives on in Mrs. Hobson, and I believe it.

PROLOGUE

I learned of Miss Fry while researching *The Jefferson Hotel: The History of a Richmond Landmark*. Her father, Peter Meriwether Fry, worked at the hotel when it opened in October 1895, took over as manager in July 1897 and ran the operations through 1910. In trying to flesh out a little bit about him for the book, I met his granddaughter, Bettie Terrell Dorsey Hobson, better known as Miss Bettie or Mrs. Hobson. She provided information about her grandfather and scrapbooks containing newspaper articles and photos. Discussion about her grandfather led to talk of her Aunt Elinor.

Elinor Fry, Richmond dance teacher from 1920 to 1970, played a significant role in the hotel's history. She starred in several balls, dances and formal events at the hotel, and her pupils performed there many times. Indeed, between Peter Fry's thirteen-year management reign—getting the hotel off to a good start and seeing it through some very difficult times—and Elinor starring in so many shows, being the "Belle of the Hotel," so to speak, I think the hotel should name a suite or conference room after her (or the Fry family) or perhaps change the name of the Rotunda to the Elinor Fry Rotunda. For that matter, the City of Richmond should name her birthday (July 23) as Elinor Fry Day and consider erecting a historical marker where her studio used to be at 2600 Monument Avenue.

Mrs. Hobson then brought out several thick scrapbooks bursting with articles, letters and photos about Elinor ("Auntie El"). Anyone who researches and writes history knows scrapbooks are gold. Someone needed to take advantage of this original source material compiled in the scrapbooks and write a book about her, an opinion I rendered (and later regretted) in the hotel book. Once the hotel book was published (by The History Press in July 2012), I decided my next project would be a book about Elinor Fry but then immediately began worrying that someone might have taken my hint and already started such a book about her. Happily, no one had or did. Mrs. Hobson shared the scrapbooks with me and kindly set up several meetings with former pupils to help in the research.

In reviewing recollections over several decades, things change, and events sometimes get recalled differently. What might have been true about the dance studio, a routine or some other incident for one dancer may have been different for another. Two dancers in the same year, even the same show, could have different memories. What might have been going on in the studio in the 1950s could be quite different from the 1960s. Bear in mind that different recollections can be both true and accurate.

Sometimes the articles in the scrapbooks had been cut out of a newspaper (or other publication) without identifying the name or date of the publication.

The Mosque was later renamed the Landmark Theatre, and in 2012 it became the Altria Theatre, but since it was called the Mosque during Elinor Fry's life, it will be called the Mosque in this book. Also, the newspapers of the day, on which I relied in much of the research, often placed "Miss" before a girl or woman's name; hence, "Miss" will frequently be used here.

Miss Fry's pupils do not call her Elinor Fry. It's always Miss Fry. Since this book is for them, I'll call her Miss Fry, too. Miss Fry deserves to have a book written about her life and accomplishments. I feel privileged to write it.

I

OUR MISS FRY

Five, six and seven decades later, her former pupils smile and tear up a bit thinking of Miss Fry. For her extensive travels to exotic lands to learn new cultures and to mega cities like Paris, London and New York, to teach, learn and get ideas for future routines; for all her talent, fame and grace (evident by just gazing at her, let alone the hundreds of newspaper articles written about her); for perhaps being the first woman licensed to fly an airplane in the state of Virginia—with all those possibilities and opportunities, the woman who could have done anything and gone anywhere assiduously returned for fifty years to the mirrored dance studio on Monument Avenue, where she lovingly tended, with discipline, but always, *always* with kindness, to her pupils, her flock, her "children." Each autumn she welcomed them back to begin lessons. She blended keen business skills with a kind heart and creative genius to produce a delightful alchemy of enchanting performances to enthusiastic audiences for half a century—a remarkable feat by any standard. Wise, elegant, smart and kind, to her pupils, then as now, she will always be Miss Fry, "Our Miss Fry."

The words vary but say the same thing: Miss Fry's love and attention proved to be among the most important things making the students who they became as adults. She taught them, indeed. But mostly, she inspired. Her lessons transcended dance; in many respects, the classes became lessons for conducting life. She would make her students proficient in dance but also nurture the lifelong value of doing the right thing, doing good. Someday the students would outgrow dance, lose interest perhaps, suffer injuries or health problems or simply age, but they should always do good and be kind to others.

She made each pupil feel special, as a politician does, but without the cunning or guile. She always found a way to compliment, even when correcting, and to complement missing skills, highlighting strengths and discreetly—no need to make a fuss or risk embarrassing anybody—conceal weaknesses or flaws. Everyone became adequate dancers (at least) because she wouldn't have it any other way. She mined the diamond qualities out of some roughs, polishing imperfections. With patience and determined discipline, she made the pupils want to practice and learn. Anyone can teach great dancers, but who happily works with the not so talented? Who teaches blind children to dance and eagerly brings them into practices and recitals, especially in a time when those with physical problems were often shunned? Who involved kids with polio—who could not stand or walk—in a show, providing a lifetime of happy memories? Why, it's easy and fun! The other pupils watched intently, learning important lessons. Miss Fry didn't have to lecture them that everyone had strengths and weaknesses and that the key to everyone's benefit and happiness was to emphasize the good things and overlook shortcomings. She didn't need to proselytize about being kind to everybody, always. She didn't have to say any of that. She lived it. For fifty years, she taught lessons like that day after day. Our Miss Fry.

Student after student remarked how fortunate they were to have known her. Constance Traylor Ackerman wrote, "A nicer person I have never met," and Mary Rolfe O'Neill Joyner said she didn't know how blooming lucky she was. Linda Salsbury Weinstein recalls the time with Miss Fry as one of the major influences of her life: "I loved her dearly." Ms. Weinstein remarked that Miss Fry had a way of making every child feel special, like she was the best dancer there.

Pupils fondly remember the cards and gifts they got from Miss Fry and how she supported and cheered them on, even outside of dance. She genuinely cared for her students. Susan Stewart Porter recalls Miss Fry showing up to watch her perform in a high school talent show, and Grace Bloxsom Cofer remembers Miss Fry choreographing high school productions. One pupil told me how much it meant that Miss Fry visited her—more than once—at the hospital after a car accident.

Pupils recall the scrapbooks in the studio, bulging with newspaper articles about Miss Fry. They looked up, and *Presto!* Their "famous" idol was holding their hands, patiently walking them through a number. The girls loved Miss Fry, worshipped her, wanted to be near her, wanted to be her. After Miss Fry

Miss Elinor Fry. *Courtesy of the Valentine Richmond History Center.*

retired, Winifred Slater Hazelton sometimes saw her at annual performances of *The Nutcracker* and loved going to the event because of the possibility she might get to see and talk with Miss Fry. She calls it "one of the best times of my life."

Claudia Wilson Pratt remembers the experience as a major part of her life, its positive impact lasting to this day: "She helped to make each of us more gracious and gave us the ability to deal with all types of people as we grew older." Wade Ogg opined that if "consummate southern lady" were in the dictionary, Miss Fry's picture would be next to it.

Pat Goldman recalls the recitals were one of the biggest things in her life, and Pamela Privette Meltzer called the experience "a large part of life for many of us." Nancy Lee Archbell Bain said Miss Fry was always an inspiration to her, even long after she stopped studying dance: "I loved her and am grateful for the great joy I found in moving to beautiful music from my earliest childhood days." Nancy Ogg Tripp said she wished she had half the grace as "this special lady." Schuyler Sneed remarked that Miss Fry was riveting and graceful. "I was shown so much and was made to feel like I could really do these things...I thank Elinor Fry for adding grace to my life."

Gale Hutzler Hargroves loved everything about the dance experience: "Even when correcting you, Miss Fry never raised her voice or got angry; she would compliment and build up your self esteem. She gave such encouragement, we were so fortunate to have encountered Miss Fry in our lives." Ms. Hargroves' aunt lived in the same building as Miss Fry, so Ms. Hargroves always eagerly hoped for a chance outside of class to visit Miss Fry.

Nancy Lynn Edwards Siford said Miss Fry, although only about five-foot-three, was larger than life. She voiced what many pupils believed: Miss Fry wouldn't let you get it wrong because she was so precise. "She was a role model, a very strong, independent woman who always helped people rise above mediocrity. She was impartial to a fault."

"The spirit of the dance slept within all of Miss Fry's pupils," remarked Bette Bloxsom Witherington, "and all she had to do was shake it awake. Miss Fry had infinite patience. She never gave up on a person. [The dance studio] became the focus of some of my happiest childhood memories."

Barbara Elizabeth Crowder Jensen recalls that after the first class Miss Fry knew all the students' names—every one. "She was a graceful legend, who taught young people how to turn body language into useful exercise and bring strength and beauty into daily lives. She is blessed to be remembered by so many who loved her."

Becky Yonan clearly remembers the night after one particular practice, sitting alone on the front porch steps of the Monument Avenue studio, waiting for her dad to pick her up. All the other children had already gone home. Seeing Becky alone, Miss Fry took her around the corner to get ice cream. Becky was nervous that she would miss her dad when he did arrive, but Miss Fry assured her it would work out, and it did. Ms. Yonan cherishes the memory of the "very special" Miss Fry and the unexpected ice cream treat.

Harriette Kent said just being in Miss Fry's company was a privilege, and to know your child was being taught by a master teacher with a warm,

Miss Elinor Fry. Miss Fry started teaching dance in 1920, the same year she graduated from St. Catherine's. *Courtesy of St. Catherine's School.*

gracious personality was on par with having your child accepted to a top-rated college. There was always a waiting list for her classes. "Getting the call that your child was "in" was a very special day."

Jana Privette Usry said that in many respects, she modeled her life after Miss Fry. According to Ms. Usry, Miss Fry went for the "total package," that is, everything about her—personally and professionally—was positive, meticulous, crisp and clean. The pupils idolized and worshipped her. She exuded so much love. While in school, Jana had to do an oral presentation about China. For the presentation, Miss Fry happily offered her a kimono brought back from China.

The dancers recall the end of practice, which concluded with a curtsey, and then running up to Miss Fry's outstretched arms for a big hug. Many remember the special treat of doing a somersault at the end of practice for Miss Fry, who would be right there to guide or catch those needing assistance. They'll never forget the birthday parties, which took on the same joyful tradition each time: everyone sang happy birthday and the birthday girl got a cupcake with a candle, a pretend spanking, her face gently squeezed by Miss Fry and then a kiss. The other children got lollipops. In the 1940s, the birthday child got an "all-day sucker," solid caramel on a stick that took more than a day to dissolve. It may not sound like much when it's reduced to printed words on a page, but seeing the smiles every time this little snippet was retold makes it clear it meant an awful lot. Our Miss Fry.

STUDENTS WHO STAYED IN DANCE

Of the thousands of pupils Elinor Fry trained in half a century, perhaps none went on to greater success in the entertainment field than Virginia (Patsy) Garrett. Patsy Garrett was born to a show business family. The boxer Jack Dempsey was said to have weighed in on her name, enthusiastically proclaiming that the baby looked like a Patsy, not a Virginia. After studying for Miss Fry for fourteen years, Ms. Garrett moved to New York in 1938 to join Fred Waring and his Orchestra, becoming his featured soloist and comedienne. In the 1940s, everybody in America knew of the famous Fred Waring. The popular musician and bandleader had his own radio show and television show, a blender named after him and the sobriquet, "The man who taught America to sing."[1]

After becoming nationally recognized, Ms. Garrett returned many times to Richmond over the years to participate in charity events (with her sister Frieda) and the annual Frylics. In September 1953, she returned to do the radio show *Here's Patsy!*

She signed a contract with MGM and ended up with a long career in show business, starring in more than thirty TV shows and movies, including *Ben Casey, Kojak, Maude, The Waltons, Columbo, Benji, Room 222* (six times) and 1987's *Dennis the Menace*, in which she played Mrs. Wilson. From 1974 to 1981, she played the "chow-chow-chow lady" in Purina Cat Chow commercials, which featured her doing a little dance. She told me that Miss Fry sometimes called her during that time to tease her about still remembering her dance skills from the lessons on Monument Avenue. As of late 2012, the ninety-one-year-old Patsy Garrett was performing *Saturday Radio Matinee*—sketches of old radio shows—at a senior theater center in Palm Desert, California.

Other pupils also went on to careers in dance or entertainment. This list is not all-inclusive. The earliest pupils to move on might have been Emily Thompson, Anita Wyland and Hertha Bryant, who danced their way onto Broadway in the late 1920s. In June 1928, Misses Wyland and Thompson traveled to New York with Miss Fry and Miss Fry's mother. They tried out, were accepted by the Keith-Albee dance company and immediately signed contracts to perform in the musical *Along Broadway*. Four months later, the professional dancers—with their names changed to Jean and Elaine de Ville—returned to Richmond while *Along Broadway* played at the National Theatre. In December 1930, having concluded a vaudeville tour, Miss Jean de Ville danced at the Sunny South Food Show at the Mosque. A later story reported that she became an RKO movie star. Wyland and Thompson danced at various Richmond events, including the Ladies' Night "Grotto" at the Elks Home in February 1927 and at Washington and Lee University's Fancy Dress Ball the following year.

Viewers of Frylics' shows from the mid-1930s would have been surprised to know that little Tommy Wolfe would go on to become one of the best writers of American literature. The author of *The Right Stuff* took lessons from Miss Fry and danced in *Mr. and Mrs. Is the Name* and *Merry-Go-Round*. In *Merry-Go-Round*, children dressed as ponies and drivers. Tommy Wolfe, along with little Billy Terrell (Miss Fry's nephew) played drivers.

In the late 1930s, when the San Carlo Opera Company made its annual stop in Richmond, the troupe contacted Miss Fry for assistance in finding a two- or three-year-old to fill the role of Cio-Cio-San's child for its production of *Madam Butterfly*. Miss Fry didn't have a tot that young to recommend,

Miss Fry started giving dance lessons from the basement studio at 2600 Monument Avenue in October 1923. This photograph is from about 1935. *Courtesy of Bettie Terrell Dorsey Hobson.*

but she had the next best thing: Suzanne Branner, who although older than requested, happened to be very small (thirty-six inches tall) for her age and, most importantly, could dance and take direction well. The San Carlo Company agreed and gave the undersized Suzanne the experience of performing in a professional opera production. One of the pictures in Elinor Fry's old scrapbooks shows the pint-sized Suzanne standing next to Kay Frances, a pupil who stood over six feet tall.

Mary Todd and La Verne Lupton transitioned from students to professional dancers. Mary Todd performed at Loew's in February 1938, and La Verne Lupton danced in *The Show-Boat Follies* at the National Theatre in July 1939. According to the website playbillvault.com, Lupton danced on Broadway in the early 1940s in *Too Many Girls* (with Desi Arnez) and *Star and Garter.*

Also making the transition at about this time was Edith Wray, who in 1940 was named "Radio Queen of the South." Shortly afterward, she began dancing and singing with Wally Stoeffers' Orchestra, and by May 1942, she, Wally and the band had a month-long gig at Tantilla Garden. Wray, who began dancing with Miss Fry at age six, was eighteen at the time.

Edward Markward changed his name to Mark Ward when he made the move from Richmond to Broadway in 1950. One story reported that he danced in *Gentlemen Prefer Blondes* and *Pal Joey*. According to the website playbillvault.com, he also performed in *Damn Yankees* and in Rogers and Hammerstein's *Carousel*.

Eileen Lawlor, who started with Miss Fry at age four, moved to New York in 1966 and danced briefly for the Radio City Music Hall Ballet Company. She performed in Guy Lombardo's *The Arabian Nights* on Broadway, in *How Now, Dow Jones* and in Richard Roberts's *Show Boat*, which toured the United States and Canada.

Sandra Walker performed in operas all over the world. A December 1987 *Richmond News Leader* story reported that she was on her way from Europe to Richmond to perform as the soprano soloist for the Richmond Symphony's Messiah.

Ruth Ann King joined the New York City Ballet in 1959 and stayed with it for a decade. She started lessons at age two with Miss Fry. Among other credits, she danced on Broadway in *No Strings* (selected by the composer Richard Roberts out of a field of five hundred dancers) and in *A Midsummer Night's Dream*. Because she was only fourteen at the time, she had to report regularly to the Society for the Prevention of Cruelty to Children to prove she wasn't being abused. When *A Midsummer Night's Dream* was performed in Washington, D.C., Miss Fry flew down from New York City to watch it, and her husband, Stuart Phillips, came up from Richmond.

Fifteen-year-old Lynda Beran made her professional debut in the New York Ballet's *The Nutcracker* in December 1966. According to the *Capital Times* (of Madison, Wisconsin), the Beran family moved from Richmond to enroll Lynda in the New York Ballet. The story noted that Lynda Beran took dance lessons in Richmond from Elinor Fry and Marion Mease. In the 1950 Frylics, Beran danced in *When They Played the Polka*.

Cornelia Connell, a former Rockette and assistant instructor for Miss Fry, danced in *Soaring* in the 1970 Frylics with Miss Fry and her other assistants at the time: Mary Rolfe O'Neill Joyner, Bettie Terrell Dorsey, Marie Pendleton Brook and Odessa Pregeant Brooks.

Deborah Smith was selected Miss Teen-Age Richmond in 1968 and competed for the national title. She spent several summers with professional companies and at the age of sixteen had received a full scholarship with the Joffrey Ballet for the following summer.

John Hurdle danced in Broadway's *Call Me Mister* and on tour with *Annie Get Your Gun*. In the late 1960s, after leaving dance, he became director of Ringling's Circus Museum in Sarasota, Florida.

Patricia Lee Goldman started with Miss Fry at age six, moved to New York at thirteen and danced in New York, Philadelphia and various European cities, for companies such as Les Ballets De Monte Carlo, formerly Ballet Russe De Monte Carlo.

Pamela Privette Meltzer took dance lessons from Miss Fry from the age of two to eighteen. She left Richmond immediately after high school and

Linda Salsbury at barre. *Courtesy of Linda Salsbury Weinstein; photo taken by Adolph Rice Studio.*

in the next four years performed with the Ballet Company of New York and danced professionally in many shows, including *Gentlemen Prefer Blondes*, *Oklahoma*, *My Fair Lady* (with Ray Milland) and *Autumn's Here*. She also acted in several television commercials and modeled clothes. Because of dance, she became interested in health, which led to writing and reviewing health and beauty articles as an editor for *Parent's* magazine.

Roger Riggle Jr. (www.rogerriggle.com) has made a career in dance and entertainment. Currently, he directs and choreographs musical operas and teaches dance for the Olney (Maryland) Ballet. As this was being written, Roger was heading to South Africa to put on performances of *South Pacific*.

Jacqueline Goldberg Jones (www.jacquelinejones.net) has made a stellar career in the entertainment field with a long list of accomplishments and awards. She performs frequently in professional stage productions, most recently *Death of a Salesman* and *Steel Magnolias*.

Romy Nordlinger (www.romynordlinger.com) is another former student with an impressive resume, with roles in popular television shows (like *Law and Order: Criminal Intent*), in regional and New York theater and in film.[2]

Some people claim Shirley MacLaine took lessons from Miss Fry, but from what I can tell, it appears doubtful. My attempts to contact Ms. MacLaine to ascertain this have been unsuccessful, but I didn't see her name (Maclaine or Beatty) associated with Miss Fry in any documents, Frylics programs or newspaper articles. Of course, proving a negative is difficult. Mrs. Hobson told me she once got a call from MGM asking for photographs or film of Shirley MacLaine, which suggests MGM might have believed MacLaine had been a pupil of Miss Fry's. Put this in the category of unlikely but uncertain.

Peter Meriwether Fry

A biography, even one about a woman's life in dance, would be incomplete without some family history, so here it is. Frances Elinor Fry (Frances was seldom used, except in legal documents) was the third and last child (born on July 23, 1903) of Peter Meriwether Fry and Irene Virginia Hancock Fry. Peter and Irene were married on June 15, 1897, precisely two weeks before Peter ("P.M. Fry") took over as manager of Richmond's Jefferson Hotel, where he had been employed as chief clerk since it opened in October 1895. Before that, he had worked at the Greenbrier (White Sulpher Springs, West

The Jefferson Hotel. Miss Fry's father managed the hotel from 1897 to 1910. *Courtesy of the author.*

Virginia), the Albermarle Hotel (in New York) and the Hotel Fairmount and the Lookout Inn (both in Tennessee).

The two children born to Peter and Irene before Elinor were Peter Meriwether Fry Jr. ("Meriwether") and Jane Virginia ("Virginia") Fry. Virginia married William Amonette Terrell. Bettie Jane Terrell Dorsey Hobson is their daughter. The Frys lived at the Jefferson (as was the custom for hotel managers in those days) until 1903, when they moved to a house next to the hotel.

Peter (March 24, 1856–January 22, 1911) and Irene Fry (March 11, 1873–February 6, 1957) are buried in Hollywood Cemetery.

The Fry family has long and noble roots in Virginia's history, going back to a grandfather, Joshua Fry, the first professor of mathematics at the College of William and Mary, and a close friend and associate of both George Washington and Thomas Jefferson.

II
LEARNING AND TEACHING

Miss Ella Binford's Star Pupil

Under Miss Ella Binford's tutelage, Miss Fry started dancing young. In August 1906, barely three years old, she performed as Little Miss Muffet in a Mother Goose costume party in Natural Bridge, Virginia. From then on, she couldn't stop. She was performing at the Jefferson Hotel at the age of five, and her seventh birthday party was held at a posh resort, which the society page called "the charming event of the week." Before her teenage years, she performed at carnivals, fancy dress balls and a vaudeville show called the *Blues' Bazaar*, where she won a prize for her fox trot and for perhaps the first rendition of what became her signature dance: a Swan Dance. At age twelve, she performed at least three times—in just the spring of 1916 alone—at the Jefferson Hotel: in a *Skirt Dance*, a toe dance called *The Hesitation* (under the auspices of Belle Bryan Day Nursery) and a *Shadow Dance* with Gwendolyn Seldon. The adorable little Elinor Fry and Gwendolyn Seldon, one witness reported, "simply brought down the house." The article reported the fun the dancers had at the party, "pelt[ing] each other with confetti and all sorts of unique favors." With this early success, it's no wonder Miss Fry made dance her life.[3]

The performances and accolades went on and on. Before age eighteen, she performed many times at the Jefferson Hotel, participated in another vaudeville show (*The Snowball Minstrels*) and danced in plays written by Richmond's own James Branch Cabell (*The Rivet in Grandfather's Neck* and

The Jewel Merchant) staged by the Little Theatre League. The big event of her youth might have been *Toyland*, a recital put on by Miss Binford's pupils. With a cast of 150, this May 1919 performance to benefit Sheltering Arms Hospital was "one of the biggest amateur affairs given in Richmond for many years." This big-bash recital became a staple for many dance teachers, including, years later, Miss Fry.[4]

Around 1919, the stories started referring to Miss Fry as a pupil of Miss Idear Traylor and Miss Margaret Anne Boyer, not Miss Binford anymore. A 1920 advertisement mentioned that Miss Binford had been teaching for eighteen years. She was born on July 25, 1879, died on June 15, 1945, and was buried in Hollywood Cemetery. Decades later, girls named Jean Binford and Katherine Binford took lessons from Miss Fry.

MISS TRAYLOR, MISS BOYER: TRAY-BOY STUDIO

Sometime about 1912, Idear Steele Traylor started teaching dance to pupils in Richmond, Fredericksburg and Petersburg. She was born in Petersburg, Virginia, in 1884. The 1920 census shows her living in Fredericksburg as a boarder with a man named Bradley and his thirty-four-year-old daughter. In about 1919, Miss Traylor and another dance teacher named Miss Margaret Anne Boyer formed the Tray-Boy School of Dance, with Miss Fry and Miss Berkeley Davis as the first graduates in April 1923. In addition to their star pupil, Miss Fry, Tray-Boy also taught other girls who became dance instructors, including Julia Mildred Harper, Ruby Chapman, Corlease Wells and Cleiland Donnan. Mothers sent their children to learn dance from Miss Traylor, and those students often ended up sending their children and so on. The *Danville Bee* reported in September 1934 that Traylor and Boyer were in Danville at the time giving lessons. Miss Boyer eventually opened her own dance studio in Danville.

Starting in 1918, Misses Traylor and Boyer staged annual recitals called the Tray-Boy Follies. The *Halifax Gazette* (South Boston, Virginia) reported in June 1927 that the Tray-Boy Follies had become so famous that people traveled from all over the state to see them. For the 1930 show, 120 dancers (50 from the Richmond studio and 70 from Fredericksburg), including tots as young as three, performed nearly forty numbers. With colorful, attractive and original costumes, the entertainment was reported to be "a brilliant exhibition of talented dancers." Little Miss Fry danced in five Tray-Boy recitals at the Strand Theatre, to benefit the Florence Nightingale Circle of Sheltering Arms Hospital (the Mosque didn't open until 1927), including *Polly Prim* in 1919 and *The Goose Girl* in 1921, in which she performed many roles—as Princess Shielda, as an "Icicle" in a number called "The Christmas Trees," in "Storm" and in the finale, "American Beauty Ballet." One reviewer acclaimed her "exquisite grace as a toe dancer," and another noted, "With artistic success [her] grace and exquisite dancing" held the entire audience. *The Goose Girl*, billed as a musical extravaganza, boasted 300 pupils. Also in the show were Grace Slater, Virginia Lee Hooker and Janet Turpin. The program listed the dances, dancers and advertisers in a format very similar to Miss Fry's later Frylics recitals.[5]

November 1921 found Miss Fry dancing and skating as "Jack Frost" in the four-day musical extravaganza called *The Merry Wheel*, hosted by the Academy of Music. Costumes were made in New York. She also played Zaftah in a number called *Legend of the Idol's Eye*. Her performance, according to a review, was "one of the most beautiful things in the entire performance...[She] covered herself with honors in [her] wonderful toe dancing. [The] splendid exhibition of her dancing...was much applauded."[6] Also in the performance were Miss Virginia Donnan, Estelle Dennis, Miss Helena Caperton, Norman and Mrs. Norman Call and Horace Gans (who was in the Polo Dance). The prize for the first night's performance (audience members who donated a penny could cast a vote) went to the Polo Dance. She also appeared in Tray-Boy's *Land of Joy*, the troupe's annual offering for 1922. In that show about Japan, she performed as Princess Yum Yum.

The Ziegfeld Follies invited Miss Fry to audition, and the Keith-Albee circuit offered her the premier danseuse role. But she didn't want to dance professionally, despite the opportunities.

In May 1922, she played the Spirit of the Virgin Land in the Virginia Historical Pageant, a role she "won" as a runner-up in a statewide vote to select the queen for the Adventure Days Pageant. Newspapers across the state carried ballots that people could cut out and mail in. Voting took place from September 15 to October 15, 1921, with fifty-five contestants to choose from, from all over the state (but twenty-five of the fifty-five were from Richmond). Forty-four contestants were listed as young women, the other eleven as matrons. Winning as queen was Mrs. Harry Semones, the wife of a Roanoke doctor.[7]

She performed in 1922's *Crystal Ball* at the Jefferson Hotel. "Sixteen of Richmond's most attractive girls", the newspaper reported, "will dance with all the abandon and spirit of the holiday season."[8] In 1922, Misses Traylor

"Soaring," *left to right*: Suzanne Carter, Jane Bralany, Miss Fry, Marjorie Adams and Baretta Oliver. *Courtesy of Bettie Terrell Dorsey Hobson.*

and Boyer gave awards to some of their five hundred students. Miss Fry won for expression and Greek dancing. The last time Miss Fry was referred to as a pupil of Miss Traylor might have been in November 1922, after her performance in *Ocean at Sunrise.*

Miss Fry danced in *The Venetian Princess* in 1923, in which it was reported she "again delighted Richmond audiences" with a "charming toe solo"; in a 1923 vaudeville show called a *Public Phund Phest* (Miss Fry danced in "The Slave Girl," "Valse," Snowflake Ballet" and "Magic Pipes of Pan"); and in 1924's *Signal Fire,* which was performed in Richmond, Danville, Norfolk, Lynchburg, Petersburg and Charlottesville. The Danville newspaper called her "one of the most gifted toe-dancers."[9]

In the early 1920s, she performed in the American Legion–sponsored annual revues such as the *Frolics of '23*, in which the paper reported she was "widely known as one of the most gifted dancers in Richmond." Boasting nearly one hundred in the cast, this Strand Theatre production featured one number with girls dressed to represent powder puffs, calling themselves

FRYLICS *of* '47

Sponsored
by
Central Committee of The American Legion
and the
American Legion Ladies Auxiliaries

Frylics program, 1947. With the exception of four years during World War II, Miss Fry hosted the annual Frylics every year from 1933 to 1970. *Courtesy of Bettie Terrell Dorsey Hobson.*

"The Powder Puff Girls" (Virginia Terrell and Virginia Donnan were in this number). The newspaper remarked that the show was led by local stars of recognized talent such as "the delightful Miss Elinor Fry."[10]

Another grand vaudeville bash in which Miss Fry performed was 1924's *A Ballet of Winter* at the Academy of Music for the benefit of Sunnyside Nursery. She danced in "Orange Grove," a California scene. The *Times-Dispatch* called this revue—starring more than 150 boys and girls, some as young as three—"the big olla-podrida of entertainment."[11]

Miss Fry took lessons over the years as often as she could on just about every aspect of dance or other activity she might weave into a routine. Patsy Garrett recalls Miss Fry getting step dance lessons from Richmond's legendary Bill "Bojangles" Robinson. Bojangles taught Miss Fry on a platform with three or four steps, which she subsequently demonstrated to her students, who then performed the routine in the Frylics of 1935.

Although she started teaching in 1920, she didn't open her own studio until October 1923. A newspaper article reported that she had taken a group of rooms in the basement at 2600 Monument Avenue and transformed them with touches of blue and green. "There is a nature room bare save for a long mirror to teach the small pupils...It is a tiny place—just a beginning, but it is quite a feat for a debutante of last season...[This] dainty slip of a girl...revealed herself as a business woman of the first order."[12]

THE STUDIO AT 2600 MONUMENT AVENUE

At 2600 Monument Avenue, Miss Fry immediately began her lifetime passion of running a dance studio, enrolling and teaching pupils and organizing practices and recitals. She often taught students for free if their families were having financial troubles. Perhaps she recalled her own youth, when she had to temporarily stop taking lessons at the age of eight because her father died and the family couldn't afford lessons.

Through the 1920s, she hosted several teas at her studio, for Misses Dorothy Meek, Hildreth Scott, Virginia Archer Page, Mary Bell Miller, Cordon Fry, Margaret Burwell and Barbara Grundy, to name a few. She instructed all types of dances over the years. An advertisement from 1934 reveals she was teaching classes and private instruction in tap, musical comedy, ballet, interpretive, acrobatic, soft shoe, character, German and ballroom dancing. A reviewer noted that the Frylics demonstrated "versatility in tap, military tap, soft shoe, drumstick tap, fast toe strut, and Indian folk dance."[13] And the jitterbug. The 1953's *Say It with Flowers* recital included the "Jitterbug." Almost sixty years later, Linda Salsbury Weinstein, who danced in the number, is winning awards in jitterbug contests. "Dancing meant everything to me," she says, "and still does."

> *Say it with flowers*
> *Beautiful flowers;*
> *Orchids and roses for you.*
> *Perfumed posies heavenly hued,*
> *Gardenias or heather*

Will tell you whether
He'll be your man of the hour
So, say it with a beautiful flower.

The first time children were identified in newspaper accounts as pupils of Miss Fry may have been in December 1924, when several of her students danced at the Academy of Music's *Black Cat Minstrels* to benefit the Elks' Basket Fund. At the Strand in 1925, her pupils performed a Russian Dance in the *Frolics of '25*. An account reported a performance of her pupils Anna Massei and Lucille Andrews. Miss Massei later became a Richmond dance instructor.

In February 1925, two of Miss Fry's pupils, Floyd Ward and Marvin Powell, danced at the Winter Garden, Hotel Richmond. The article reported that Ward lived in Lynchburg and traveled to Richmond for lessons. So at least by the age of twenty-one, perhaps earlier, Miss Fry (who turned twenty-two on July 23, 1925) had pupils coming in for weekly instructions from places as far away as Lynchburg.

As of 1933, the annual recitals became known as Frylics, but years earlier the shows were called various names, including "Miss Fry's Dancing Dollies."[14] The recitals appear to have started at least by 1927, for on December 29 of that year, Miss Fry and twenty-six of her dancers, ages three and a half to sixteen, performed in a New York–style revue at the Mosque, with acrobatic, Grecian dances, the Waltz Clog, the Military Buck and a toe dance. In February 1931, they presented a cabaret at the Mosque and then were

Miss Fry was perhaps the first woman licensed to fly an airplane in the state of Virginia. She never flew again after her brother's airplane crash in June 1931. *Courtesy of the Valentine Richmond History Center.*

back again in November 1932 for a revue sponsored by the Elks. Both times they were simply referred to as Miss Elinor Fry's s dancers.[15]

For the record, she changed the name of her studio in 1938 from the Elinor Fry School of Dancing to the Elinor Fry School of the Dance. Also for the record, the saddest day for the studio and its pupils might have been October 15, 1938, the day Ray Francis, a former model, pupil and Miss Fry assistant, was left paralyzed from a car accident while returning home from a Duke football game. She had danced in the very first Frylics number, *Moonlight and Roses*, and a year before the accident had performed a specialty dance at a Tantilla Garden Halloween party. Four months before the accident, the newspaper published a photograph of her modeling a bathing suit. The good news is that she transitioned from a wheelchair to a newly and specially devised brace and cane, eventually making her the first person to do so.[16]

St. Catherine's class photo, 1920. *Left to right, back row*: Helen Sauer, Elinor Fry and Nannette Ford; *front row*: Elizabeth Guy, Grace Shepherd and Margaret Upshur Brown. *Courtesy of St. Catherine's School.*

Miss Fry taught some two-year-old tots (the youngest was twenty-seven months), but she believed the ideal age to start lessons was three. Babies younger than that, she believed, usually had concentration and coordination problems.

She began teaching in 1920, the same year she graduated from St. Catherine's School. Her original six pupils swelled to hundreds over the years, and when she retired in 1970, the number was up to about seven hundred with a staff of twenty-one. In the fall of 1924, the *Times-Dispatch* reported that upon her return from New York, she would be opening a studio at 2805 Monument Avenue. For whatever reasons, this move from 2600 to 2805 Monument did not occur. Also never occurring was Miss Fry converting a lot she owned on Mulberry Street into a dance studio. Although she owned the lot for years and had planned to design a studio, it never happened, for reasons lost to history.[17]

Lessons usually started in early October and ended a couple of weeks before the recital, usually in early May. Miss Fry taught all day long, from about 9:00 a.m. to 12:30 p.m., with an hour off for lunch and then back to lessons until 9:00 p.m. Classes began promptly as scheduled and were based on age, with youngsters earlier in the day. With its large mirrors, the studio seemed electrifying to a child upon first entering. Winifred Slater Hazelton said that all the mirrors made it feel exciting, like she was in New York City.

A cardboard cutout of dancers. Students cut out paper while waiting for classes to start. *Courtesy of Bettie Terrell Dorsey Hobson.*

Bette Bloxsom Witherington remembers descending the stairs to the basement and entering a whole new world. She and the other pupils loved rummaging through the large box of outgrown ballet slippers, toe shoes and tap shoes, looking for a pair that fit and trying to remember which shoes went with the costumes. Upon first descending the stairs, you entered the waiting room. Off to the left side was a small closet and to the right, a bench. If students got to class early, they could fold pieces of paper as Miss Fry had shown them and cut out figures with scissors.

A big rectangular post with a barre on each side and decorated with framed Degas ballet paintings was at the center of the room. Many dancers recall the post as circular, but that might be because they went around it so many times.

Miss Fry read the roll; the pupils curtsied. Practices started with ballet slippers, warming up, stretching at the barre and putting on tap shoes. Next, they formed a circle around the center wall and proceeded to shuffle and then do basic tap steps. Toward the end of class, the assistants rolled out two long, heavy mats to practice summersaults and tumbling. For many, this mat work was the most fun part of practice. Another training device was the rolling pin, a heavily padded rod held by two assistants, which allowed students to practice backbends and walkovers. Various tools were utilized over the years, including a parachute held on the outside rim by the pupils. As they lifted their arms, the parachute rose, and they would all run under it into the center and then back out.

The fragrance of cookies baking, courtesy of the Southern Biscuit Company (later FFV) a block away, pleasantly streamed in through studio windows.

The lessons were hands-on, meaning Miss Fry and her assistants physically walked pupils through the number if necessary, so there was no way it wouldn't be learned, even by pupils who were not very coordinated or musically gifted. In addition to the regular cadre of instructors, Miss Fry occasionally brought in ballet specialists she had met in New York. Many pupils recall a French-speaking man, and others recall Mr. Sergev, a Russian ballet master.

For the days leading up to the recital, students were forbidden from doing anything active for risk of injury. Parents were asked to put kids under a "glass case" so they would be healthy and not have bruised-up knees. Rehearsals were often at Tantilla Garden, Benedictine High School or, in the early years, at the Mosque or the Elks Club auditorium. In the very early years, the few dancers could rehearse right in the studio.

Miss Fry called the tall girls her big girls, and the little girls were her giants. She didn't allow gum chewing. Pupils were prohibited from leaving or going into the audience with their costumes on during a rehearsal or recital. She said things like her girls "didn't sweat, they perspired" and, to motivate the pupils in stretching, "That hurts so good." In later years, Miss Fry also had a dance studio in the basement of her house at 301 Greenway Lane, where she would serve desserts to her assistants after the Frylics shows. Although it's in a residential neighborhood, Miss Fry was grandfathered in to teach dance there. The prior owner (Margot Johnson) had set up the studio in the basement and had taught dance. The Elinor Fry School of Dance gave lessons from both locations for several years. Students at the Greenway Lane studio may remember her feline mascot named Pas de Chat (a ballet move that translates from French to "cat's step") prancing through the studio like she owned the place.

Other Richmond Dance Studios

Misses Binford, Traylor and Boyer continued teaching dance for many years. They and their students ended up occasionally bumping into one another—and into Miss Fry and her pupils—at various events. In November 1925, Misses Binford, Traylor, Boyer and Fry were named committee members for the upcoming Ballet Russe. In June 1926, pupils of Miss Fry and the Tray-Boy studio took part at the City Auditorium commencement of Mrs. Mattie Ridout Atkins' Music School.

Students of various dance studios competed in April 1931 in the Tournament of Arts at Thomas Jefferson High School. The winning performance ended up being a tie between an acrobatic group from the Elinor Fry studio and a military buck trio from Tray-Boy studio. Overall honors went to Marion Mease, a pupil of Miss Fry who went on to run her own dance studio from about 1949 to 1990. At the same competition the following year, Miss Fry's pupils swept virtually all the awards. Lucille Stoddart of New York was one of the two judges. More about her later.

Over the years, there was no shortage of dance studios in the Richmond area. Pupils from Miss Fry's studio, as well as Julia Mildred Harper's and Tray-Boy's, performed *Dance of the Blessed Spirit* at the Mosque in December 1933. They were back the following December exhibiting a waltz with the Richmond Symphony Orchestra. One of the bigger extravaganzas bringing the studios together might have been October 1950's *Tobaccorama*, where audience members witnessed Miss Fry's pupils doing a can-can and the Martinique School performing an Arabian dance. These were followed by a Vienese number by Idear Steele Traylor's dancers, a Scottish number by Margot Johnson's dancers, a Mexican number from the Chapman School and a South American number by Arthur Murray dancers. For the finale, the Julia Mildred Harper School performed the *Richmond Blues*.[18]

Much like the Frylics, many of these studios also hosted grand recitals. In the spring of 1934, for example, Tray-Boy put on *Silver Slippers*, and Ann Massei's troupe performed *Magic Carpet* at the Mosque. On May 24, 1952, the Margot Johnson School of the Dance exhibited *Footlight Parade* to benefit the Rheumatic Fever Fund. In June 1947, Julia Mildred Harper's dancers performed *The Talk of the Town*, with Jack Kaminsky leading the orchestra, to benefit the Polio Treatment Center.

Other studios included the Howle Fisher and Annette Baird Dancing Studio, Charlotte Miller School of Dancing, the Elcorise School of Dancing (the name formed by the first letters of the owner's three names: Miss Elmer Corinne Iseman), the Isobel M. Robertson School of Dance, Mary Virginia Myers Dance Studio, the Olaker School of Dance, the Dance Studio of Etta Johnson and Marlise Bok, Betty Jane Whitlock, the Marion Mease School (with Carolyn Seal, accompanist), Huband's, Astor, Beck's, Wells and the Mary Marshall Garrigan School. As of May 1948, former Fry pupil Alice Hafling Armory had her own dance studio in Charlottesville. Her pupils were presenting a revue that month called *Tomorrow with You*. Currently, in Glen Allen, Virginia, Cecelia McKee Marano, a former Fry pupil, runs the Glen Allen Dance Center and hosts recitals each April at the Cultural Arts Center with profits donated to the Shriner's Children Hospital. Ms. Marano's studio is what became of Miss Fry's studio after Miss Fry retired. For a brief period between Miss Fry and Ms. Marano, Margaret Woodburn, a Fry pupil and assistant, ran it under the name Heritage School of the Dance.

A 1961 advertisement reveals that Traylor changed the name of her studio (at least the Petersburg studio) to the Idear Traylor Mayes School of Dance. When she closed her Richmond studio in 1964, she had fifty-six "grandchildren" and eleven "great-grandchildren" of pupils she once taught. She continued dancing until 1967, died in October 1968 and was buried in Petersburg's Blandford Cemetery.[19]

There's a Traylor Dance Academy in Colonial Heights, Virginia, run by Miss Traylor's great-niece Constance (Connie) Traylor Ackerman. She took lessons from her great aunt but eventually also took tap lessons from Miss Fry because Miss Traylor wasn't teaching tap.

Parents could take their children to one of many Richmond studios, but for many there really was no choice other than Miss Fry's. They had all heard about Miss Fry, even if they didn't have a family member who had taken lessons. Jacqueline Viener summed it up succinctly when asked why she took her daughter: "Miss Fry was an institution; it never would have occurred to me to take her to anyone else."

A letter in the scrapbooks from August 1954 reveals that one mother asked Miss Fry to take her four-year-old daughter as a student: "It would break my heart to have to send Elizabeth somewhere else." In the same letter, the thirty-seven-year-old woman asked Miss Fry for lessons for herself and a couple of her friends.[20] This may have been the inspiration for the "Mother's Class," which started in the mid- to late 1950s. Several mothers learned modern dance routines and performed in various numbers. A *Mothers' Day Cards* dance from the 1960s featured mothers and daughters performing together, including Debbie and Zelda Markel and Virginia Ogg and Nancy Virginia Ogg.

DANCE IDEAS FROM FOREIGN TRAVEL

In a sense, Miss Fry's dance studio was like a geography course but without the homework assignments. Pupils learned about the culture of foreign lands. They didn't just read about people wearing different clothes; they actually got the opportunity to wear them in dance numbers.

Miss Fry's international travel was announced in the papers and became the source of many Frylics dances, which often included authentic clothes and props, such as real wooden shoes from Holland or robes from China.

Japan in the summer of 1930; China in 1933; England, Paris and Italy in 1934; Mexico in 1935; Europe in 1936; Bermuda in 1938; and Guatemala in 1941. Her files include a note from the Society of Teachers of Dancing thanking her for her demonstration. While in London, Miss Fry, along with seven other American teachers, danced the "Sizzle," which the *Daily Sketch* called "a new version of the Negro style dancing."[21]

She recycled the routines over the years in various Frylics, often with different names but pretty much ending up the same way: spirited and talented children rendering a "foreign dance" in the clothes of the people from that country and singing the songs that people in that country might sing. So Dutch dance numbers, for example, came up again and again over the years in various themes. They might be included in routines about foreign cities, like the 1939 Frylics about the New York World's Fair that took place that year. That show had a number called "The Artist Quarter," which included Ellis Schwab impersonating an artist, the "Artist Quarter of Paris" (with a song by Barbara Angell), the "Latin Quarter" and the "Spanish Quarter," in which twelve girls—six of them dressed as boys—performed "La Rosita."

Dutch dances often made it into routines about dolls, a common staple of the recitals. In fact, you would be hard-pressed to find recitals without dolls. The 1947 show, for example, carrying the theme "A Modern Department Store," featured different types of stores one would find in a department store, including a toy department, and just like that you have all types of doll routines, such as "Bavarian Dolls," "Irish Dolls," "Scotch Dolls," "China Dolls" and "Russian Dolls." Marjorie Branner Adams, who had studied at Julliard, sang "At the Balalaika" in Russian costume.

The 1963 Frylics also portrayed foreign dolls, with separate dances for "Irish Dolls," "Dutch Dolls" and Scotch, Hawaiian, Swiss, Spanish, Chinese, Japanese, Indian and East Indian Dolls. The 1966 show included "Mexican Dolls," "Dutch Dolls," "Ballerina Doll" (played by Donna Ellen Tyler) and "Irish Dolls."

In the finale of the 1950 show, a Dutch dance number was included in the larger act about airplanes flying to foreign lands. Dressed as airplanes, dancers made a round-the-world tour with stops in various places, including Holland, conveyed to the audience in numbers called "It's Tulip Time in Holland" and "Jeanette and Her Wooden Shoes," with children performing in the real wooden shoes Miss Fry brought back from Holland.

This round-the-world journey included stops in Scotland (where they did the "Hop Scotch Polka"), Ireland ("My Wild Irish Rose"), Switzerland, Russia (excerpt from *Swan Lake*), Poland and Africa. They even traveled "South of the Border," where Anne Hunter danced "a striking and intricate number."[22]

The Frylics of 1935 included "Going South," a number featuring the Lewis sisters dressed as hotel bellhops. "Their gay good humor," the newspaper reported, "will make everyone wish to stay in their hostelry."[23]

As for traveling south, the 1936 Frylics included "Jarama," "Los Viejitos" and "Jarabe Tapatio," a Mexican number performed by Miss Fry and a man from Newport News, Virginia, named Joseph Bryant. The *Times Dispatch* carried a photograph of Peggy Mease, Alyce Ann Finke and Gentry Horton wearing sombreros for their number.

Miss Fry (right) obtained dance ideas from her travels. *Courtesy of Valentine Richmond History Center.*

Travel came up again in the 1959 Frylics, with children "flying" to Mexico, Switzerland (where they did the "Swiss Polka," "Edelweiss," "Swiss Misses"), Greece ("Greek Folk Dance") and even some unidentified lands in the western United States, where "Cow-Boys" and "Cow-Girls" danced the "Western Round-Up."

Tulip Time in Holland reappeared in 1953, this time with "A Little Dutch Girl and a Little Dutch Boy" and "Tiptoe Through the Tulips." Other

Miss Fry performing "Swan Dance."

dances included "Blue Bells of Scotland," "Swiss Floral Festival," "Oriental Poppies" and "Persian Market."

To the performers in May 1953, the foreign countries became places they felt they knew something about, however remote and distant. Ireland wasn't just Ireland anymore; it was the place that would always make them remember, with a smile and a laugh, singing and dancing "My Wild Irish Rose" or "The Irish Boogie." To a child dressed in a glittering creative costume, in a well-trained troupe, cavorting and frolicking to live music and to an enthralled audience, on stage at the grand Mosque, it meant something. Indeed, travel and geography could be great fun.

Dutch numbers could have come into the Frylics, as in 1958, in a dance about "Languages," with routines about the Spanish (with numbers called "Senoritas" and "Matador") and the French ("French Gendarmes," "French Maids" and "French Bonnets").

They could have come into the show simply as "Travel," as in 1959, in which dancers "visited" various countries around the world, or they could have found a perfect fit in 1962's *Out of This World*, the recital coming a mere three months after John Glenn's flight into orbit. In that show, performers orbited over various countries, so there were dances for "Orbiting over Africa," "Orbiting over Paris," "Orbiting over Persia," "Orbiting over Holland" and "Orbiting over Scotland." Each number boasted children dressed as locals of that country, singing tunes from that country. It was like a Halloween party—a massively captivating and educational Halloween party.

Miss Fry demonstrated immense creativity in using different themes to represent foreign cultures. In 1955, *Carnival in Venice* provided the hook, with clever numbers such as "Gypsy," "Persian" and "Polka," while 1956 included *Scenes of the World*, highlighting "Spain," "Haiti" and "Scandinavia."

Dutch dances could have come in, as they did in 1957's *Songs of the Islands*, a show devoted to islands around the world, including the "Isle of Marken," a place Miss Fry had personally visited. A mid-1930s newspaper

Scottish dance—Gale Hutzler. *Courtesy of Gale Hutzler Hargroves.*

article reported that when Miss Fry toured Holland, she visited the Island of Marken in the Zuider Zee, where citizens wore elaborate costumes. So it was only a matter of time until those colorful clothes and street scenes made it into the Frylics with numbers like "Dutch Girls and Boys," "Tiptoe Through the Tulips," "It's Tulip Time in Holland" and one of Miss Fry's favorites, "Jeanette and Her Wooden Shoes." Tulips were never far from Miss Fry's heart. They reappeared in 1962 with Jacqueline Diane Goldberg as one of the dancers in "It's Tulip Time in Holland" and Debra Margaret Markel in "Tiptoe Through the Tulips."

In one Frylics, about 150 children—including tots as young as three—waltzed in wooden shoes in the "Dutch Garden." The "Islands" theme included "Hawaii" ("Hawaiian Bamboo," "Liquid Sunshine," "Song of Old Hawaii"), "Cuba" ("Red Hot Peppers," "Senoritas"), "Trinidad" ("Takes Two to Tango," "Calypso"), "Sicily" ("Sicilian Polka"), "Alcatraz" and "Ireland" ("Irish Colleens," "Wild Irish Rose"). Winifred Ann Slater was an "Irish Colleen," as was Jean Barron. Jean's aunt and uncle came up from Southern Pines, North Carolina, to see the show. The next day, they sent a Western Union telegram to Miss Fry congratulating her: "Words are inadequate to describe the Frylics of 1957. We enjoyed it very much."[24] The show also included "Bondage" with Lina Lee Bacigalupo, Bettie Terrell Dorsey and Cheryl Joy Ahern, a dance repeated several times over the years. The dance's theme related to people around the world freeing themselves from the chains of fear and oppression and living happily together in peace.

The shows featured many foreign lands, including some countries that no longer exist, such as Tyrol (in the Swiss Alps) in the 1937 show, with Gilbert Gray Henley singing a Tyrolean number.

According to the *Times Dispatch* in May 1935, the older girls in *The Dragon* wore glorious Chinese robes and coats, boasting richly embroidered dragons, mice and other strange creatures with "eyes of jewels that glisten as their wearers move in the strange dances of the celestial empire of an older day."[25] Miss Fry brought the costumes—reportedly more than two centuries old—from China in 1933, and a local shop (the article did not name the shop) displayed them in a window for several days.

Patsy Garrett recalls the Chinese dragon scene. Each of the eleven dancers dressed as a dragon, but when they entered the stage, they were all covered to make them appear as one big dragon. Since Patsy was the smallest, she ended up being the dragon's tail. The stage resembled a Chinese village, and the big dragon slowly snaked its way across, through the village. When it got to the other side of the stage, the music abruptly changed, and *poof!* The magic dragon transformed into eleven small dragons, each slithering back to the other side of the stage. Miss Fry devised routines like that year after year.

The 1935 show included a number with fourteen girls dressed as French maids, each pushing a baby carriage. What a surprise for the audience when a very young child jumped out of each carriage to join in the dance!

Routines about foreign countries could make it into the show, as in 1960, in a number about holiday cards, so *St. Patrick's Day Card* would bring in songs and dances like "Too-Ra-Loo-Ra-Loo-Ral" and "The Luck of the Irish."

Routines about foreign countries fit perfectly during World War II. In 1942's *Allied Nations*, separate dances were done for "South Americas," "Maracas" (which included "La Cumparsita"), "Song and Dance" by Edith Wray, "England," "China," "Russia," "Greece," "Dutch" and the finale, "We Are All Americans."

The creativity was not so much in depicting foreign places but in *how* they got into the shows. With or without Miss Fry's travel, there would have been Irish, Spanish and Dutch scenes in the Frylics. They were obvious ideas for dance numbers. Dances about foreign places were going on long before Miss Fry visited Europe and probably went back to the Tray-Boy recitals, vaudeville shows and whatever came before that. But going there personally, selecting and bringing clothes and props back and sending postcards and letters (at a time when very few people traveled internationally) gave the dances real pizzazz and oomph. It wasn't just about Holland; it was belly-laughing fun about real places their own cherished Miss Fry had personally visited, with the real wooden shoes and postcards to prove it. Whoever thought geography could be so entertaining?

In April 1934, a show (not directed by Miss Fry) called *A Pageant of Nations* took place at the Mosque. Several groups were impersonated, including Germans, Indians, French (Miss Fry's pupils sang and danced the French Marseillaise Hymn), Syrian, British, Greek, Italian, Czecho-Slovakian [*sic*], and Negro (with something called "The Negro National Anthem").[26]

The Frylics of 1970 included a "Swiss Festival" and a Hawaiian number, "Song of Old Hawaii":

> *There's a perfume of a million flowers*
> *Clinging to the heart of old Hawaii*
> *There's a rainbow following the showers*
> *Bringing me the thought of old Hawaii*

There's a silver moon, a symphony of stars
There's a hula tune and the strum of soft guitars
There's a trade wind sighing in the heavens
Singing me a song of old Hawaii

MABEL PUTERBAUGH

Miss Fry's most frequent travel companions were her mother and her friend Mabel Puterbaugh. Newspapers reported Miss Fry's travels and often noted she was traveling with Puterbaugh, a friend she met in 1930 onboard a ship traveling to Japan. Eighteen years older than Miss Fry, Puterbaugh was from a wealthy oil family and spent her life traveling and collecting antiques. She wanted to run an antique shop, but her family wouldn't permit it. Each spring, Miss Puterbaugh came to Richmond for the Frylics and helped out with the preparations. The society page of the *Hutchinson* [Kansas] *News* reported in April 1933 that Miss Fry and Miss Puterbaugh were guests at a buffet and swimming pool party in Hutchinson. Four months later, the *Los Angeles Evening Herald and Express* reported that Miss Fry and Miss Puterbaugh were in town. While in Los Angeles, Miss Fry performed at the Women's Athletic Club. The article added that Miss Fry had "somewhat deserted the ranks of society, and has devoted much of her time to the arts, particularly interpretive solo dancing."

The *Hutchinson News* reported in July 1941 that Miss Puterbaugh and Miss Fry would be in town for an upcoming wedding. Afterward, they took a vacation to Denver. In 1951, they were reported to be enjoying the winds and sands of Hawaii. That same year, a New York dance publication reported that Mabel Puterbaugh was the oldest nonmember attendant of the Dance Congress.

Mabel Puterbaugh, Miss Fry's friend and frequent travel companion. *Courtesy of Bettie Terrell Dorsey Hobson.*

The publication added they would both be back for the following year's Dance Congress.[27]

Mabel Puterbaugh was born in Hutchinson, Kansas, on January 18, 1885. At various times over the years, she was listed as a resident of Hutchinson; Malakoff, Texas; McAlester, Oklahoma; and New York City. She never lived in Virginia. She died on March 19, 1961, and was buried in Hutchinson.

New York City

Sometime about 1924, Miss Fry began making annual summer or early fall trips to New York City, originally to take dance lessons, later to teach other instructors and, finally, to have her pupils perform.

In August 1924, she and her mother spent almost a month in the city—where Elinor took lessons at Denishawn Studio, under the direction of Ruth St. Denis and Ted Shawn. Six months later, dancers from Denishawn's were in Richmond performing at the City Auditorium. Within days, the papers carried a photograph of a portrait of Miss Fry that had just been painted by Carl Clarke, president of New York's Fine Arts Syndicate. It was not stated whether this was a commissioned work or something Mr. Clarke painted on his own.[28]

Each year, usually in late August, the papers reported that Miss Fry was leaving for New York, and then two or three weeks later there was another mention that she had returned home and would be reopening her studio in early October. A newspaper notice from 1925 reported Miss Fry and her mother would be moving into their new house at 317 West Grace Street upon their return from New York.[29]

Sometimes the notices included a little more, such as the type of dances she studied in New York— Spanish, Oriental, special ballet, musical comedy—as well as who accompanied her, usually her mother, sometimes Mabel Puterbaugh and sometimes a student, such as Mary Todd in 1927. The 1927 notice added that Miss Fry was "well known for her grace and artistry and admired beyond Richmond."[30] Occasionally, the notices mentioned other cities, such as Chicago, where Miss Fry served with the Chicago National Association of Dance Masters.

Miss Fry and her mother were in New York on June 28, 1931, when they got word that Peter "Meriwether" Fry Jr. (Miss Fry's brother) had died in an airplane accident. Known to friends as "Skeeter," the thirty-two-year-old man-about-town's airplane crashed while taking off from Charles Field, headed for a debutante party in Washington, D.C. The plane crashed on Bellevue Avenue. Fry was dead when reached by Charles Ancarrow, in whose yard the plane fell. Charles Field was located near today's A.P. Hill Monument, at the intersection of Laburnum Avenue and Hermitage Road.

In New York, Miss Fry also selected materials for the Frylics' costumes and scenery. Her 1939 trip must have been especially exciting because the Frylics that year was devoted to the New York World's Fair. Approximately 350 children sang and danced to an array of events related to the fair and to New York City, so everything took on a special meaning. By that time, Miss Fry was a seasoned traveler who had made New York City her home away from home for at least fifteen years. One paper called the upcoming Frylics an "ultramodern stage picture."[31] New York popped up several times over the years in recitals. The 1956 show included *Pleasure Trip to New York*, with numbers "Chinatown," "42nd Street," "Rockettes," "Central Park," "Yankee Stadium," "Shopping on Fifth Avenue," "Greenwich Village," "Night Club," "Entertainers" and "United Nations."

In the early 1930s, Miss Lucille Stoddart of New York City, a judge for the Richmond Academy of Arts dance contest, was so impressed by a number performed by Miss Fry's students that she (Stoddart) asked Miss Fry to teach it to her dance instructors in New York.

In a Richmond dance contest two months later, Shirley Cadmus and Marion Mease received the tap-dancing prize. Stoddart and Gerald Hanchet (of Grand Rapids, Michigan) were the judges. Of course, Miss Stoddart was well aware of Miss Fry's dance skills at that point as she (Stoddart) had been one of the two judges for the 1932 Beaux Arts Ball, an event in which Miss Fry stole the show with her grace, beauty and dance skills.

Beaux Arts Balls took place in Richmond from 1931 through 1933. Thirty governors attended the April 1932 extravaganza at the Jefferson Hotel and saw Miss Fry—"the Spirit of the Ball"—descend at the stroke of midnight from the ceiling in a mammoth and modernistic rounded carriage that was supposed to resemble a tulip.

Miss Fry started teaching in New York City in August 1932, when she received the first of several certificates from Stoddart's dance studio. Perhaps the handful of certificates in the scrapbooks are just a few she chose to keep, like the one from 1951, when Lucille Stoddart (her title was "Directress") recognized Miss Fry for her appearance in the Dance Congress convention held for American and Canadian teachers. Miss Fry participated with several other New York dance groups, including the Dance Educators of

America. In the 1950s and 1960s, She served as an officer for some of these organizations, including as first vice-president for the American Society of Teachers of Dance in 1963.

In 1948, at the seventieth annual convention of the American Society of Teachers of Dance, Miss Fry "a sturdy teacher of capers,"[32] led her fellow instructors through "Sunbeams," "Till the Clouds Roll By" and "The Drum Dance." According to the *New York World-Telegram*, she put them through "a stern curriculum for anyone over sixteen." The article referred to Mrs. Elinor F. Phillips's (married in 1941 to Stuart Phillips) specialty as baby dances.[33]

The Dance Educators of America held its twentieth-anniversary convention in July 1952, with Miss Fry listed as teaching baby dances. The Lucille Stoddart Dance Congress hosted its annual convention in July 1950 at the Hotel Commodore, with a sixteen-page newsletter to promote it. Registration cost fifty-five dollars, which included the banquet. Instructors were Ernest Carlos (tap styling), Frances Cole (children's ballet), Elinor Fry (children's work), Jimmy Sutton (stylized tap), Vesper Chamberlin (baton group novelties), Al Gilbert (children's work) and Alei Ramov (ballet for children).

Miss Fry sometimes took her pupils to New York to perform, and they were always well received. A Dance Congress publication remarked that the *Swiss Bell-Ringer* was a smash hit. A "delightful group of 100 mothers and fathers, 100 children came by bus from Richmond to honor the Dance Congress with an exhibition of two of the finest drills it has been our privilege to witness."[34] As if bringing one hundred students wasn't enough, Miss Fry also brought a Smithfield ham for Miss Stoddart. The children are, Miss Stoddart opined, "typical of what we think of little Southern beauties and their deportment was charming and unobtrusive at all times."[35]

A July 1955 article reported forty-eight teenagers had just left Richmond to represent the Elinor Fry School of Dance at the Dance Congress. The group demonstrated the "Confederate Rifle Drill," the Hawaiian "Hula" and "Patriotic Fantasia," featuring a manual of arms that would "ring a bell with any serviceman."[36] Staff sergeants from Fort Lee coached the students on correct procedure. "Parents wished bon voyage and issued last minute instructions and several hopped aboard to make the trip too."[37] Patsy Bickerstaff recalls the costumes—not surprising since her mother, Doris Bickerstaff, was one of the seamstresses. For the drill, the girls wore gray jackets, gray kepis, gray satin pleated skirts lined with red satin and, underneath that, red tights. For "Patriotic Fantasia," they each had costumes of red, white and blue; the colors presented to the audience changed as the dancers moved about in the routine.

Dance Educators Convention. Miss Fry went to New York City every year to take dance lessons, teach dance lessons, have her students perform and buy supplies for the Frylics' costumes and scenery. Her Richmond dancers were invited to appear on *The Ed Sullivan Show. From left to right:* Jane Sydney Green and Linda Salsbury. *Courtesy of Linda Salsbury Weinstein.*

Former pupils fondly remember performing and sightseeing, including watching a Rockettes' show, *The $64,000 Question, The Gary Moore Show* and a private midnight screening of a movie about a ballet dancer called *Red Shoes*. A midnight movie in New York City! Think of that thrill for a minute. Some students took ballet lessons in New York, and several were invited to audition for the Rockettes. Miss Fry's group was even asked to perform for *The Ed Sullivan Show*. Ed Sullivan called and wanted to bring the drill to his show, but the group had to return home. Miss Fry had no feasible way to quickly let parents in Richmond know or to get their permission for the dancers to extend the trip. Long-distance calls, readers over fifty will remember, were very expensive.

The students did art projects in their down time, cutting out windows of buildings in black paper and then laying yellow paper behind it to make nighttime scenes in New York. Some mothers went along on these New York trips but few fathers. The newspaper reported that Dr. and Mrs. James Galloway took their children, James Jr. and Anne, in July 1950. James

Galloway attracted a little notoriety of his own back in Richmond in the early 1950s, performing his "Scottish Sword Dance" around town. Although he did not take lessons from Miss Fry, he appeared in several Frylics numbers, including "Charleston" and "Top Hat Strut."

Dr. Galloway wanted to stay at the Chelsey Hotel (rather than the Hotel Gorham or the Algonquin, where the group usually stayed in the 1950s) because that was where his family had stayed upon emigrating from Scotland. All the dancers would agree with Claudia Wilson Pratt's summary: "What an exciting experience it was!"

Miss Fry also did some royal dining in New York. In October 1957, a group called the Pilgrims and English Speaking Union invited her and her husband to a white tie dinner at the Waldorf-Astoria in honor of Her Majesty Queen Elizabeth II and His Royal Highness, the Prince Philip, Duke of Edinburgh.

III
SETTING THE STAGE

The Mosque (now known as the Landmark) Theatre's inaugural program took place on October 28, 1927, with its opening performance the next day. Prices were twenty-five to seventy-five cents. It boasted five thousand seats and a Wurlitzer triple-manual organ, installed at a cost in excess of $50,000. Shortly afterward, Miss Fry and her advanced pupils ("lithe and graceful children") participated in *Jazzmania* at the Mosque, a venue, according to an advertisement, "run by the people for the people." Miss Fry, "regarded as one of Richmond's ablest dancers," performed in six numbers, including the scarf dance finale.[38]

On May 29, 1933, Miss Fry's dancers staged their first annual recital at the Mosque, or at least the first recital called Frylics. Except for a break during World War II—when the pupils performed to raise money for war bonds—the annual recitals continued (always at the Mosque) through 1970. For a while in early 1940, there was some doubt about a show that year because the transfer of the theater to the city was being completed, and until that was done, no shows could take place. To house all the dancers and their mothers, who served as "dressers" and "wardrobe women," Miss Fry needed the capacious Mosque; no other venue provided enough space.

Other studios held recitals at the Mosque, too, but by the mid-1950s, most of them had gone to recitals every two or three years or had moved to smaller venues, like high school auditoriums. A *Times-Dispatch* article by Edith Lindeman in March 1958 estimated that about nine thousand children, from ages three to eighteen, were taking dance lessons in and

From the 1936 Frylics program—Miss Fry and her students. *Courtesy of Bettie Terrell Dorsey Hobson.*

around Richmond each year. But despite that interest, the big recitals were losing steam. The reasons:

Wear and tear on the teachers, who have to get new ideas, create costumes, select materials, arrange for dressmakers, figure which children will fit into which numbers, choreograph according to the ability of the children, arrange rehearsal times, find rehearsal space, pick out music, get an orchestra, arrange for ticket sales and oh, you name it.[39]

The cost for putting on a show had soared, to somewhere between $1,200 and $3,000. The dance studios got nothing for the performances (all profits were donated to charity) and sometimes took a financial loss.

At the time of her retirement, Miss Fry mentioned that cost and the difficulty of getting such a large number of students together for rehearsals were big factors in ending the Frylics.

Contracts in Miss Fry's scrapbook revealed she paid $26.24 for insurance at the Mosque in May 1962. Renting the building from the Department of Recreation and Parks for two rehearsals in April 1967 cost $100.00.[40]

Frylics were on Saturdays, so the schools released students early to get to the Thursday or Friday afternoon rehearsals on time. A note to parents in 1947 stated that Mr. Willet, superintendent of schools, agreed to let children be excused if they had a note. Father O'Connell also excused parochial school pupils in time to get to the rehearsals.

Miss Fry kept parents advised of schedules and activities, a very impressive feat given she had about three hundred pupils in the 1930s and about seven hundred by 1970. The *Times-Dispatch* carried a notice in April 1940 that Miss Fry would be at the John Marshall Hotel to meet with the pupils' mothers and would do a dance for them, too. She sent notices each year with instructions for rehearsals and recitals. The 1963 ticket for dress rehearsal:

This ticket will admit one pupil and parent (or maid) to the Dress Rehearsal, Thursday, May 2, 1963. The rehearsal will start at 3:45 and all who are in Act I, must be at the Mosque IN COSTUME ready to start PROMPTLY.

Those who are only in Act II, will not have to be ready to start until 5:00 o'clock, unless they wish to come early to watch the first act. NO ONE is to go into the audience in costume EXCEPT DURING DRESS REHEARSAL. On May 4th, the Matinee will start promptly at 2:15, so please be at the Theatre by 1:15, if you are in The Opening Scene. The Evening performance will start at 8:15, please be in place by 7:15. Please remember there is no parking on Main Street after 4:00 o'clock. Towing enforced.[41]

COSTUMES

Three to six hundred children usually performed in each year's recital, requiring thousands of yards of exquisite materials for the handmade costumes. There were reported to be about 1,500 costumes in the 1936 Frylics, 2,000 in 1937 and nearly 1,800 in 1938.

Hill Brown, formerly the minister of Grace and Holy Trinity Church, recalls the "costumes, fabrics and happy activity" at 2916 Monument Avenue, the house where Miss Fry lived with her mother, sister, nephew and nieces until she got married in September 1941. Dr. and Mrs. Galloway, who lived two houses east of 2916 Monument Avenue, cheerfully stored and distributed costumes and materials from their house.

The costumes had to be designed "from the severe military coats to the gossamer softness of the silver ballet and swan costumes."[42] Once Miss Fry drew the designs, she then had to purchase the materials and fabrics. Some costumes included beads, sequins, elaborate hats, belts and various other accessories. Miss Fry, her mother, her sister and some of the "sewing mothers," including Jessie Corey, cut and placed the fabrics and materials for each costume in a bag so mothers could conveniently pick the bags up and sew the costumes or make arrangements to have them sewn.

Edith Lindeman notes, "A mother whose child is really to be a blackbird can come to the studio, see the costume, and take home with her in a bag into which Miss Fry has placed all the necessary materials-silk, buckram, feathers and two big buttons for eyes."[43]

Bette Bloxsom Witherington said Miss Fry's mother (whom the students referred to as Nana, Mrs. Fry or Grandma Fry) "presided over rooms filled with gorgeous fabric, beads, trimmings, spangles in every color imaginable." Suzanne Branner Kessler recalls that Nana cut patterns for the costumes, and "you had to stand still till she fitted them properly." Patsy Garrett recalls being intimidated by Miss Fry's mother, a strict disciplinarian. Miss Fry's mother would sit in the back row at the rehearsals (where there were no microphones), urging the children to sing louder.

Patsy Bickerstaff says her mother, Doris Bickerstaff, a true artist in her own right, was in awe of Mrs. Fry's creative ability:

[Miss Fry] would design the costumes for recitals, and "Nana" would figure out exactly how the costume should be made. She was a brilliant seamstress, and could look at a child standing across the room, pick up a newspaper and a pair of scissors, and cut out a pattern which, when used to put together a garment, would fit the child perfectly.

The strict disciplinarian and highly dignified Nana had a soft side many didn't see. She was not above sharing a risqué joke on occasion and loved eating heaps and heaps of a sugarcoated puffed wheat cereal called Ranger Joe.

And then the rush to sew. According to a 1930s newspaper article, "Within a few weeks mothers will begin their customary spring orgy of costume-making...all of which are made in the homes of the young dancers or by dressmakers working under the eagle eye of each mother."[44]

Some children were in several numbers, up to six or seven per recital, while others (often because of the cost of the costumes) were limited to one or two dances. In addition, younger dancers—usually with lesser skills—were generally in fewer dances. In 1955, Edith Lindeman noted:

An effort is made to keep the costumes within reason. Costumes...if made at home, are held down to $4 or $5, those for older girls will cost more... sometimes last year's costumes can be used in this year's play by changing the color, adding or subtracting a skirt or a headdress or turning a long ballet skirt into a short one and coloring the whole thing with sequins. This is hardly feasible for some of the older girls, since the most adept teenagers... will wear out their costumes by doing benefit shows all during the winter.[45]

Three years later, Ms. Lindeman reported that costumes rarely cost less than $3.95 and could run as high as $10.00 to $15.00.

The bulk of the sewing was done by a handful of mothers, like "Mrs. B." To the students, her last name (Bacigalupo) was seldom mentioned and her first name (Edythe) almost never. Miss Fry spent considerable time in Mrs. B's basement working on costumes and ideas for costumes. Mrs. B and other mothers furiously sewed and sewed to get the costumes—of all sizes and styles—done in time for the recitals. The well-prepared and precise Miss Fry wanted them finished with time to allow for changes and unexpected problems. With her basement in the far west end of Richmond completely taken over for sewing, Mrs. B—a night owl to begin with—would stay up all night sewing. Some of the other seamstresses included Mrs. W. Carlyle

Carter, Mrs. Roy Hancock, Mrs. McDonald, Irma Lee Hardie and Mrs. Aylor. By any measure, they all did an extraordinary job.

Along with Mrs. B, Mrs. Bickerstaff often cut out patterns from newspapers for the other mothers. She sometimes stayed up very late, leading to punchiness the next morning. One morning the paperboy showed up, and

Frylics program, 1960. The dances were topical, educational, clever and amusing. *Courtesy of Bettie Terrell Dorsey Hobson.*

when advised that he was at the door, Mrs. Bickerstaff—with brain glazed over from an all-night sewing marathon—replied, "Put a cover on it and put it in the refrigerator."

One costume was sewn and modeled by one pupil for Miss Fry and the others. It was especially exciting if you were the one who got to wear the original costume and show it off, a thrill assigned for a while to Mrs. B's daughter, Lina Lee, or to Nancy Lynn Edwards Siford, Lina Lee's good friend. Seeing the costumes you'd be wearing in the recital was an exciting event. Miss Fry, ever meticulous, might change something on the costume at this point, perhaps adding a belt or a scarf.

Cecelia McKee Marano recalls a costume in which a long skirt was pulled up, and the inside of it looked like a man with a spectacle in his eye. The costumes for 1951's "Apple Blossom Festival" had a flower sewn on the inside, revealed to the audience when the dancers pulled up their dresses.

Edith Lindeman noted there weren't many boys in the recitals, especially after they got to Boy Scout age, when they usually dropped out of dance lessons. But those under Miss Fry's tutelage didn't mind performing if "decked out as cowboys, Indians or in junior editions of daddy's dinner jacket." Girls, Ms. Lindeman added, kept up lessons until they went off to college and got married, and "sometimes even the married ones came back."[46] Miss Fry gave separate lessons for the boys and girls, with the boys on Saturday mornings. Wade Ogg recalls about eight to ten boys taking lessons in the mid-1950s. For the most part, the boys took lessons in tap or acrobatic only.

A *News Leader* article in July 1965 reported that the students went to Clothes Rack to find their own personal rags on the Rack's rack for the hobo number. "Dressed in raggle taggle top hats, tuxedos, patches, and everything under the sun, the group was a real show stopper."[47]

The young dancers were thrilled to put on makeup and costumes, and many remember the excitement of going on stage after the show to collect tinsel, foil, glitter and sequins that had fallen off the costumes. One can easily imagine some of that treasured tinsel safely tucked away today in old scrapbooks.

It's easy for former dancers to remember the color and designs of their cherished costumes. "My debut was to be as a butterfly, and to this day, it is one of my favorite symbols. I thought I had wandered into fairyland," Bette Bloxsom Witherington recalls.

My class was divided into butterflies and blue birds. My costume had a gold lamé bodice, with yellow silk "wings" attached by elastic to the arms. The headpiece was a gold band surmounted by gold antennae. The day of the revue, I thought I was gorgeous with my butterfly costume and Shirley Temple curls…The costumes were wonderful, always in good taste, never gaudy.

And they were treasured. Debbie Howard Perkins recalls she and her sister, Ginger Howard Schiffner, used to play in their costumes for years after the recitals.

Sometimes the students modeled clothes in fashion shows around town. In April 1925, Miss Fry's pupils participated in a dance and fashion event at the Richmond Hotel's Winter Garden, to raise money for the Sheltering Arms Free Hospital. In the 1930s, the students modeled clothes on various occasions, including at a Thalhimer's fashion show in March 1930 and at the Byrd Theatre two months later. They participated in fashion shows in 1937 at the Jefferson Hotel and at Miller & Rhoads.

Prices and Programs

Ticket prices for Frylics in the 1930s were $0.50, $0.75 and $1.00. They increased after World War II to $0.94, $1.50 and $1.75 (federal and city tax included) and to $1.00, $2.00 and $2.25 by the final 1970 show. For most of those years, tickets could be purchased in advance at the Mosque, the Jefferson Hotel, the John Marshall Hotel, People's Drug Store and Levinson's Cigar Company. Parents would stand in line very early to get the best seats for the performances. A colorful program came out each year, listing the various dances—often fifty or sixty—and the names of the dancers in each number. Individuals and businesses bought advertisements. For the 1964 program, W.H. Cowardin Sons Jewelers paid $150.00 for the back cover. A full-page ad cost $100.00, unless it was on the inside cover, which cost $125.00. Advertisements came in all sizes, all the way down to $7.00 for one-thirtieth of a page and $1.00 to be listed as a patron.

Gerald Lisman, the Frylics' photographer, took out an ad in 1964 announcing he had a set up a studio in the Mosque Ballroom for Friday and Saturday afternoons. For six dollars, parents could buy three color photos of their children in costume. As a point of reference for the value of the dollar back then: in 1964, Miss Fry paid seventy-five dollars per month for the rental of her Monument Avenue dance studio.[48] The first program included an ad for Fry and Hobson Building Specialties, primarily weather stripping and roofing.

Miss Fry thanked various people, especially her assistants. Assistants in 1948 were Marion Mease, Dorothy Farley Bennett, Helen Wallerstein, Bettie Jane Terrell and Nancy Barker. By 1951, Helen Marks and Jane Thomas had joined on as assistants, and Marion Mease had departed to start her own studio. Miss Fry and her assistants posed for a picture on the cover of the 1967 program (theme: Good News), a program designed to look like a newspaper. The staff at the time included Bettie Terrell Dorsey, Helen O. Powell, Dale Adams Bowman, Margaret Murry Woodburn, Cornelia Connell, Mickey Garrett, Betty Bradley Jones, Odessa Pregeant Brooks, Cindy K. Sharp and Anna Shenfield.

She thanked the people who made the costumes, primarily Mrs. Bacigalupo, "for her magnificent work." In the mid-1960s, she thanked the narrator, Frank Soden; John Kessler and Peggy M. Binns for the artistic program covers; and Mrs. Ruth Salisbury for help with makeup. She always recognized the piano player and orchestra leaders for their valuable contributions. Henry Bryan led the orchestra for the shows from 1933 through 1946. He was replaced in 1947 by Jack "Jake" Kaminsky, who conducted the orchestra for every subsequent Frylics.

Kaminsky gave violin lessons at his home on North Rowland Street. He may have been the most popular and busy orchestra leader in Richmond in the 1940s and 1950s, leading all kinds of musical performances, including serving as conductor of the "Parking Lot Dance Orchestra" (for the "Parking Lot Canteen" at Seventh and Grace) during World War II (providing entertainment to servicemen and women) and providing the music for Colonel Stoopnagle and his Stoperoo Revue.[49] He was a very large man, likely tipping the scale at more than three hundred pounds. At the restaurant, it was not uncommon for him to devour two or three meals at one sitting. Bob Hope once called him "Skinny Ennis in reverse."[50]

Charlotte Troxell, whose husband, Mark Troxell, was the first trumpet in the band, recalls that Kaminsky would sometimes call her husband at three o'clock in the morning to go over songs for an upcoming recital. There were so many songs in the recitals that each band member had a pile of music on the floor in front of him. Band members joked that when it came to the Frylics, they didn't get paid by the song; they got paid by the pound.

Miss Fry didn't have enough money for a piano player when she first started in 1920, so her sister played the piano. Eventually, that changed, and by the first Frylics (in 1933), Helen Lindsey was at the piano, a position she kept through the 1941 recital. Carolyn Seal then took over for five years. Bette Bloxsom Witherington remarked that Miss Seal always seemed to

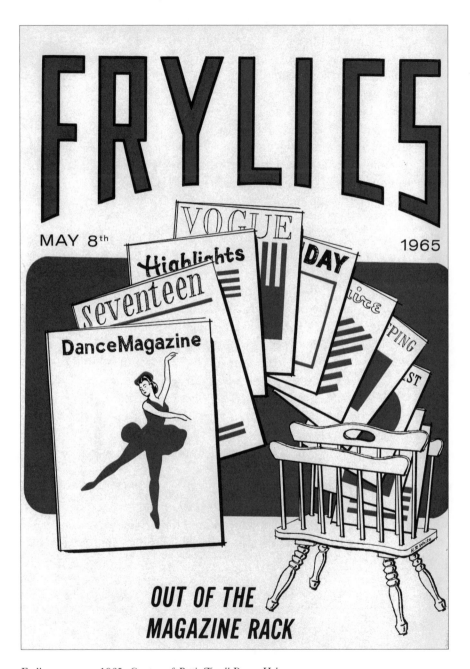

Frylics program, 1965. *Courtesy of Bettie Terrell Dorsey Hobson.*

know just how fast or slow an individual pupil could move when dancing a solo. "She never just played a tempo but seemed to tailor the pace to the capability of the dancer...and made you look good! She was tuned in to Miss Fry and they made a good team." Miss Seal left Miss Fry's production to join Marion Mease after Mease opened her own dance studio. An advertisement from September 1945 revealed Miss Fry was looking for a pianist to play classical and popular music. Full time was preferred, but part time would be considered.[51] She eventually found Alma Cilimberg (full name Alma Mae Ahern Cilimberg), who took over piano duties in 1947 and played every year through the last Frylics in 1970, sometimes with part-time assistance from Carolyn Seal or Helen Lindsey Watkins.

Heavily involved in music, Ms. Cilimberg had worked at Murphy's Music Store on Broad Street. Her son Ray recalls her performing with June Carter and the Carter Family at Fort Lee before June married Johnny Cash. He also recalls June Carter and the Carter Family coming over to the house to visit with his mother. Like Miss Fry, Cilimberg was born in 1903—January 29, to be precise. She passed away on April 29, 1977.

Cheryl Ahern Weis, a niece of Alma Cilimberg, was a student of Miss Fry's. She, like all pupils, vividly recalls how her Aunt Alma busily knitted while sitting at the piano bench but magically dropped the knitting needles and started playing again precisely when needed, without missing a beat. Pamela Privette Meltzer recalls Ms. Cilimberg's steadfastness; she seemed to be "always there." Performing in the Frylics and the experience of working with a real orchestra, according to Ms. Meltzer, was invaluable training for professional dance. The 1970 Frylics featured Alma's niece Diane Page Cilimberg in "Little Bo Peep."

Gale Hutzler Hargroves credited the piano players (who were there for every practice) and orchestra members for making the dancers perform so well. Many former students commented about how exciting it was to dance to live music. It would be rare to find live music performed for amateur productions today.

SOME ANECDOTES

The Virginia Commission for the Blind sponsored the Frylics from 1933 until World War II. On May 20, 1933, with the headline "Internationally Known Blind Woman Will Demonstrate Her Remarkable Genius," the *Times-*

Dispatch reported Helen Keller would make an appearance at the matinee and evening performances. She ended up missing the matinee because of what was reported as plane sickness but attended the evening show.[52] She spoke for much longer than anyone expected. Apparently, no one had told her there was an entire show with hundreds of children performing, and she was supposed to say just a few words. Bettie Jane Terrell, who was performing in the Frylics at the time at age two, was dressed as a pony waiting for her turn to go on but didn't make it. She fell asleep backstage as the long-winded Miss Keller talked.

Patsy Garrett recalls the blind and deaf Helen Keller being asked how she knew when to acknowledge applause. Miss Keller replied she could feel the vibrations on the stage. In one Frylics show, according to Ms. Garrett, the blind dancers accidently got turned around and performed their entire number with their backs to the audience. Miss Fry did not stop their impressive dance performance. The newspaper article about Miss Keller's visit included a photograph of Miss Fry teaching seven-year-old Dorothy Wolcott, a blind dancer.

Blind girls performed in many shows, including the 1937 recital, which featured two—Olive Coke and Phillis Lawrence—who hailed from Richmond. Their work as Swiss bell ringers won tremendous applause. The blind girls' performance in a later Dutch scene demonstrated, according to Edith Lindeman, their "unquenchable spirit…[and] Miss Fry's patience and teaching ability."[53]

Lina Lee Bacigalupo Butler recalls a child with polio participating for her therapeutic benefit. Miss Fry put the girl on a tricycle, tied her feet to the pedals and tricked out the trike with big red sequin bows, glitter and ribbons—the bigger and brighter, the better—and took the girl around the post in the dance studio. The ecstatic child loved it, could see herself moving in the mirrors, laughed and laughed, all the while building stamina and strength. Miss Fry designed a dance where all the girls lined up shoulder to shoulder to support one another, allowing this child to stand and participate in the recital.

Patsy Bickerstaff recalls a pupil with Down's syndrome, afraid to dance in the recital because she didn't think she could keep up. Without missing a beat, Miss Fry arranged it so she could stay in one place in "Old King Cole." Patsy's aunt (Anne Marie Bickerstaff), severely injured at about age fourteen and in a body cast for about a year, was told by doctors she'd never walk again; another doctor suggested dance as physical therapy. Miss Fry got her involved in dance and kept working with her. Six months later, she was walking again. Later, when Ann Marie was working in a school in Haiti, Miss Fry sent materials for costumes to help with the entertainment. Anne Marie later became Sister Anne Marie.

Mrs. Hobson recalls getting to select the song she wanted for a toe tap dance. She chose "You Are My Lucky Star." When she got home and told her mother, her mother mentioned that Bettie's father, William Amonette Terrell, used to love singing that very song to Bettie. She didn't remember any of this, as she was only four when her father passed away.

Patsy Garrett recalls that she and some other pupils were filmed on the roof of Thalhimers. When Al Jolson's *The Jazz Singer* came out in 1927, a short video clip preceded the movie at the theaters. That news clip, according to Ms. Garrett, was a video of Miss Fry and eight or nine of her pupils performing "Singing in the Rain." Ms. Garrett recalls a narrator talking about children taking dance lessons, and then the narrator focused exclusively on Richmond and Miss Fry's studio. Other early pupils recall the group making movies on the roof of the Central National Bank.

Lina Lee Bacigalupo Butler recalls losing her ballet shoes before a recital somewhere between the car and the Mosque. She was supposed to go on first. Noticing this shoe shortage, Miss Fry seamlessly rearranged things so Lina Lee came into the number at the end and thus had time to borrow another girl's shoes. What a logistical and creative accomplishment: fifty or sixty numbers with four, five or six hundred children for fifty years!

With all these dancers, unexpected things happened. Anne Hunter recalls in a number with top hats that she quickly reached to pick up the hat for Marion Mease, who had a very fast change. As Ann reached for the hat, she noticed it was filled with tissue paper. Assuming the paper was used to keep the hat in shape, she removed the paper and handed the hat to Marion, who didn't have time to examine it and couldn't do much with it at that point even if she had done so. Alas, the purpose of the tissue was to prevent the extra-large hat from sliding down over Marion's eyes. Whoops, sorry about that! Always the trouper, Marion performed the entire number with the top hat sitting on her ears and almost entirely covering her eyes.

Claudia Wilson Pratt recalls a number involving bamboo poles that resulted in her partner splitting her pants during the dance. The girls just laughed and kept dancing. Claudia and two other students liked to cut up and tried to get Miss Fry to let them do a funny dance. Eventually, Miss Fry acquiesced and let them do the "Three Little Pigs." But they had to wear pig masks. "What fun we had!" It's likely there were many split pants over the years. Sometimes these split pants left viewers wondering why pupils

Miss Fry moved into the Monument Avenue studio in October 1923. *Courtesy of Bettie Terrell Dorsey Hobson.*

sometimes danced so oddly, as when Patsy Garrett's tail didn't get pinned on right when she was the hind end of the dragon, forcing her to hold onto the tail throughout the dance to keep it where it was supposed to be.

Miss Fry let parents watch the lessons in the studio because she thought it gave students confidence to perform in front of others. But she didn't like parents talking or laughing. As the pupils were practicing their "brush-step, brush-step," a Fuller Brush salesman happened to walk by on the sidewalk outside. The studio was in the basement with windows near the top of the walls where you could see the pedestrians' legs but little else. Miss Fry had her back to the window, so she didn't know what was going on, but the mothers in the room were positioned so they could see the windows behind Miss Fry. The Fuller Brush man heard the words "brush-step, brush-step," and being a good Fuller Brush salesman, thought someone was calling for him, so he stopped and bent over, peering in the window, hoping for a sale. The mothers started giggling, and the briefly flustered Miss Fry eventually turned around and found out what was so funny. Of course, she ended up buying something from him. After Helen Powell became an assistant, parents could watch practices for only one specified week each month. Powell thought it was more difficult to teach with an audience.

During one dance, with all the children lined up and facing the audience, one particularly jocular boy —on the far left end—fell down just goofing off. Sharing in the unscripted mirth, the child next to him followed suit and so on down the line, one by one, until they all fell down. Except for the last child on the right, Lindsey, who wouldn't have any of that unacceptable silliness. Putting her hands on her hips, she sternly looked down at the dancers on the floor and scolded, "You know Miss Fry doesn't allow that!"

Anne Ball of the *News Leader* wrote an article in which Miss Fry recounted a time when two children costumed as cats somehow got their tails entangled on stage. One blurted out, "I can't—me tail's taught [*sic*]."[54]

Another time, five-year-old George Curley, who had gotten drafted into the act, ended up getting whirled madly around the stage by his slightly older cousin, Angela Brewer, "all the time fighting gallantly to restore his lost sombrero—much to the delight of the audience and even the teacher. That was the only time," Miss Fry said, "I laughed at my own children."[55]

Nancy Lynn Edwards Siford recalls one girl crying, "I don't want to be a chicken, I want to be a ballerina!"

Another chicken anecdote: One very young girl called Miss Fry the day before the recital, crying hysterically, angry she was going to miss the recital because she had come down with chicken pox. "I don't wuv you anymore," she cried. "You made me a chicken, and I got chicken pox!"

An act involving mice included a huge block (several feet high and wide) that was supposed to represent a huge block of cheese. The young children dutifully popped out of the cheese as they were supposed to, but one particularly timid girl wouldn't come out. Finally, after a bit of coaxing, she exited the cheese.

The nursery rhyme "Four and Twenty Blackbirds," performed in the 1960s, had a huge pie (sixteen feet wide and eight feet tall) descend from the ceiling.

Mr. de Veaux Riddick, designer and technical director for the Concert Ballet of Virginia—the artist who brought so much flair to many dance routines over the years—designed the set for this number. A four-foot piece of the pie slid open, and from the opening "flew" a flock of twenty-four very young children dressed as blackbirds:

> *Sing a song of sixpence,*
> *Pocket full of rye,*
> *Four and twenty blackbirds,*
> *Baked in a pie.*

> *When the pie was opened,*
> *The birds began to sing;*
> *Isn't that a dainty dish*
> *To set before the King?*

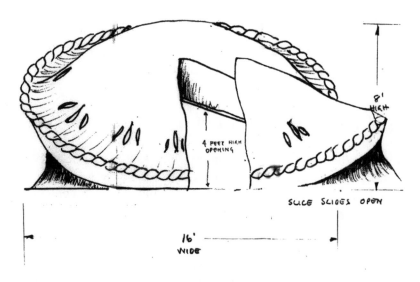

"Four and Twenty Blackbirds"—twenty-four small children flew out of a pie. The set was designed by de Veaux Riddick. *Courtesy of de Veaux Riddick.*

After one practice, about eight or nine girls went outside to wait for their rides. Being young children, they started ringing doorbells in the building, troubling up a little mischief. It wasn't long before Miss Fry came upstairs, gently put her arms around the girls and told them she had gotten a call about ringing doorbells. But, she told the girls, she had told the caller it could not be her girls because her girls would never do that. No need to scold. Simply stop the behavior. Lesson learned. (Of course, the children would not have been wearing their class leotards because they were prohibited from wearing them into or out of the studio.)

During a rehearsal in the 1960s, one of the ballerinas fell. Miss Fry stopped everything and sternly stated, "My girls don't fall." The angriest, strongest language Miss Fry ever used—and it would conjure up tremendous sadness or disappointment—was simply, "Oh, honey." All the kids loved her, but as one former student said, "We were a little afraid of her, too; you didn't want to cross the line."

Miss Fry referred to her pupils as her children, an endearing expression everyone understood and appreciated, except an unknown friendly motorist who happened to pull over to the curb shortly before Christmas 1956 to offer Miss Fry a ride. At the time, she was walking on the sidewalk laden with packages. Startled by the offer, Miss Fry managed to stammer, "Oh,

I'm sorry! I thought you were one of my children's fathers." The befuddled driver hastily drove away, no doubt wondering if the lady really said what he thought she said.

The formerly pigeon-toed Sam Hanes took dance lessons because his doctor thought it would help his balance. At the time, several reports mentioned that professional football players were improving their game through dance. It must have worked for Sam because he went on to play sports in school, earning three letters along the way. Another former dancer turned football player was Joey Smith, a big fellow who was light on his feet and an excellent dancer. Former dancer Warren Mills took his skills to the basketball court, where he excelled for the University of Richmond Spiders, culminating with a selection to the first team, all-state level. The Spiders' website today prominently refers to the period from 1952 to 1955 as the Warren Mills Era.

Harriette Kent recalls when Miss Fry told her daughter Lin the shattering news that Lin wouldn't be able to dance because the muscles in her ankles wouldn't support it. Miss Fry conveyed this bad news in such an honest, caring way that, then and now, decades later, this ballet-hopeful who was not meant to ballet remembers Miss Fry's compassion when breaking the news. Very disappointed, yes, but feelings not hurt: "Oh! If there were only more Miss Frys!"

Patsy Garrett recalls taking two trolleys with her grandmother at least three times a week to get to practice, and she could hardly wait. She especially loved the month of May because she got a double treat each year: her birthday and the recital. Patsy says she learned all her manners—other than basic table manners—from Miss Fry, who had the best manners of anyone Ms. Garrett ever knew. "Wonderful times," she says, "wonderful, wonderful times."

VERY BUSY TIMES

The spring of 1927 saw a flurry of activity for Miss Fry's pupils. In a sixty-day span, they performed at the Cathedral Boys' School for the Sacred Hearts Alumni Association, for the American Legion and at a Jefferson Hotel banquet. They danced *Cinderella* for the Children's Theatre, for a conference of the Flavoring Extract Manufacturers' Association, in the Shrine Century Ball ("in Arab uniforms and wearing the fez")[56] and back at the Jefferson

Hotel to entertain the American Pulp and Paper Mills Association. On top of that, in this brief period, Miss Fry performed as the "sweet ingénue" in James Branch Cabell's *Captain Applejack* at the Strand, where her performance was described as "especially charming...lovely to the eye, graceful, attractive and play[ed] with spirit and finish."[57] Perhaps the real proof she hit her stride by 1927 might have been that she was featured in a newspaper story about Richmond women working outside the home.[58]

May 1928 was another hectic time. Her pupils performed at the Richmond Hotel's Winter Garden, in *The Rescue of Princess Winsome* and in the grand two-day Memories of the Centuries Festival, part of "Adventure Days" in Byrd Park. Hosted by the University of Richmond Glee Club, an estimated ten thousand people "intently observed as the history of Richmond unfolded, in an event designed to capture the Mardi Gras spirit."[59]

In three months in 1929, Miss Fry and/or her pupils performed in the Shrine Circus at the Mosque, in a Colonial Ball at the Armory, at the Commonwealth Club for the American Institute of Bankers, at Washington and Lee University's Fancy Dress Ball, in a Jonas Style Revue at the Byrd Theatre, in a minstrel show, as dolls and wooden soldiers in the *Mother Goose Party* to benefit Holy Comforter Church, in *The Giant's Gumdrop* at the Women's Theatre, for a "Pink Tea" given by the Imp Club of John Marshall High School, for the WRVA Corn Cob Pipe Club, in the *Marriage of Pocahontas and John Rolfe* at Byrd Park and at a Cohen Company employees' banquet for what was called "a dance and whoopee."[60] They also performed twice for the American Legion, including a celebration where ten of the tiniest dancers sprung out of a giant birthday cake, six feet in diameter. The newspaper carried an advertisement to "Hear and See Fox Movietone News including Elinor Fry's Little Dancing Girls."[61]

Miss Fry got together with her former teacher, Miss Traylor, and together they performed for the Isodora Duncan Dancers. Her pupils danced at the Chamberlin-Vanderbilt Hotel at Old Point Comfort for the Virginia Bankers Association and on board the USS *Richmond* docked at Hampton Roads, Virginia, where the "gobs" of captivated guests, officers and crew were treated, according to the *New Orleans Picayune*, to "a real girlie-girlie show."[62] And those are just the events I found out about, in just three months. Certainly, many other performances fell through the cracks of history.

Miss Fry and her pupils danced at the Richmond Hotel (including the Golden Rule dinner in October 1925), the William Byrd Hotel (including a "barn dance" in November 1939), the John Marshall Hotel and the Jefferson Hotel dozens, if not hundreds, of times. They often performed at the Mosque (including in May 1934's *Play Fiddle Play* with Seldon Herbert), the Strand and the National (including December 1926's *A Mid-Winter Fantasy*, which the *Times-Dispatch* called "a bewitching dance specialty");[63] at high schools (including *A Southern Cinderella* at Patrick Henry School in May 1925); at colleges and churches; and at the Masonic Temple and the Academy of Music.

They performed in classical ballets and interpretive dances, musicals and vaudeville shows, including the Blue Bazaar Circus of December 1925, characterized as a "phantasmagoria of bizarre sights and sounds."[64]

Miss Fry and her dancers performed just about every chance they got. It's risky to list the groups they entertained because, invariably, many will be overlooked. They performed for business, religious, charitable, historic and fraternal groups such as the Retail Coal Merchants, the East End Business Men's Association, the Institute of Bankers, the Second Baptist Church, the Virginia Home for the Incurables (now the Virginia Home), the Catholic Theatre Guild (including in February 1941, when they danced the musical comedy hit *Rio Rita*), the Daughters of the American Revolution, the Daughters of Liberty, the United Daughters of the Confederacy and Confederate veterans' reunions (Miss Fry served as assistant maid of honor for the Thirty-second Confederate Reunion in 1922), the American Legion, the Richmond Automobile Club, the Sphinx Club of Acca Temple Shrine, the Deep Run Hunt Club's "Race Ball," the Preservation of Virginia Antiquities Association, the James River Garden Club's Flower Show (where Miss Fry performed as "Blue Bird") and the Virginia Press Association's "Gay Nineties Party" at the John Marshall Hotel Roof Garden.

They danced for the Elks and the Lions Club (Miss Fry's brother was chairman of the Lions Club Richmond chapter in the late 1920s). They danced frequently at Tantilla Garden, including performances for employees of the Railroad Athletic Association and the A&P grocery chain. They danced for workers' safety: for the Traffic Clubs of America, the National Safety Council, the Richmond Safety Council (one show was titled *How Knowledge Drives Fear Away*) and at a big bash in May 1939 to benefit industrial employees and commercial vehicle drivers, which promised a glamorous review of the Terpsichorean art (*Terpsichore*, from the Greek words "delight" and "dance," was the Greek muse of dance). Miss Fry's dancers often performed on local television in the early years of television. Because of lighting issues, the dancers were instructed to wear green lipstick.

They danced to raise money for all kinds of things, such as in May 1937, when the Chester School needed money for its piano fund; in December

"Along Came a Spider" from the Frylics of 1936. The students were instructed to look scared. *Courtesy of Bettie Terrell Dorsey Hobson.*

1936, when the Saints and Sinners Club got people to donate Christmas presents for kids; in April 1942, when the Monarch Club sought funds to buy X-Ray equipment for the Sheltering Arms Hospital; and in June 1938, when they participated in the "Bowl of Rice Revue" at the Mosque—with an estimated audience of 1,500—to aid China's innocent war victims.[65]

They performed several times for the *Swan Lake* historical pageant. The exhibition in May 1930, directed by Miss Fry (including a dance of Indian maidens), drew an estimated crowd of five thousand.

They certainly danced for local theatrical groups such as the Little Theatre. Their participation in the Little Theatre League's *In a Little Garden* was described "as thoroughly graceful and delightful as Richmond always expects Miss Fry's own dancing and that of her pupils to be. The little tots, so exceptionally well trained, as usual, drew tremendous applause."[66]

They performed at private residences, including at Bellendean, the Chesterfield County home of Mrs. Walter Scott; at Paxton, the home of Mrs. John Skelton; at the residence of Lucille Puette (for a Randolph-Macon alumni event); at the Springhill Avenue home of Miss Emma Lee Costello; and at Ballyshannon.

They performed at cultural events, such as the "Pops Concert" with the Richmond Philharmonic at City Stadium in September 1939. Three of Miss Fry's students—Karen Wyland, Deborah Smith and Anne Reynolds—danced in the Norfolk Civic Ballet's 1968 Azalea Festival.

COMINGS AND GOINGS

Miss Fry's comings and goings made news, from the time a newspaper advertisement was placed in December 1914 seeking the return of Buster, her lost small, brown and white pet bull terrier (call Elinor Fry, Madison 3950-L). In February 1917, the *Times-Dispatch* carried drawings by local kids, including her sketch of a child skating.[67]

In 1922, she was presented to society as a debutante at the opening of the German Club ("Germans" were formal dances), a brilliant function at the Jefferson Hotel (wearing a dress of white chiffon velvet with a crushed silver bodice trimmed in pearl ornaments and carrying a shower bouquet of pink roses)."[68] A couple of months earlier, she had traveled to Charlottesville for a football game and attended the *Tangerine* at the academy with Clarence Boykin.[69] Boykin was listed as the press representative for the Mosque in the theater's 1927 Inaugural Program.

Other events in later years have her returning home after a week in Frederick's Hall, where she was the guest of Miss Marjorie Terrell; going to Bar Harbor, Maine, to visit her friend Mrs. Barton Grundy (June 1926); returning from the Cascades Inn, Healing Springs; and recovering from an appendicitis operation in October 1926 (the older pupils temporarily supervised dance classes). In August 1927, the paper carried a portrait of Miss Fry (looking over her left shoulder, head tilted back) painted by someone named Von Jost, and her and her brother Meriwether's flying interests were reported. On September 17, 1929, only two and a half years after Charles Lindbergh's famous flight across the Atlantic, she received authorization from the Department of Commerce, Aeronautics Branch, to fly as a student pilot. A week later a photograph of the young aviatrix standing next to an airplane appeared in the newspaper. On November 1, 1929, right after the stock market crashed, she sailed smoothly through her "Aeroplane Dance" at the John Marshall Hotel for the Second Annual Governor's Ball. The costume was a real humdinger; real aeroplane wings appeared to have replaced her arms. A story from April 1930 reported that she would soon have her pilot's license.

The *Los Angeles Herald and Express* reported in August 1933 that Miss Fry had become an ardent aviatrix, held a pilot's license and often piloted a plane in Richmond.[70] The truth is, according to Mrs. Hobson, she never piloted a plane after June 28, 1931, the day Meriwether died in the airplane tragedy.

ANNUAL CHRISTMAS PARTY

Each year, starting at least by 1932, but possibly earlier, Miss Fry hosted a dress-up Christmas party for her pupils, usually at the John Marshall Hotel, in the very early years at the Jefferson Hotel and in some of the later years at the Cavalier Arena. Although parents and guests were invited, the party, with all its favors and fun, was for the children. Mrs. Hobson remembers Miss Fry and the assistants blowing up balloons, all five hundred of them, and they didn't have a machine to help inflate them. Advanced students put on a little show at the party, and sometimes Miss Fry performed. During the 1938 party, the children watched Miss Fry perform *Sleeping Beauty* and saw a Technicolor movie of themselves from their dance recital of seven months earlier.

Children at another Christmas party got to watch a movie of themselves from earlier in the year at Maymount. Imagine how enchanting it must have been for children back in the 1930s, long before any of them had seen a video image of themselves—as futuristic as science fiction. Indeed, every girl must have thought she was Shirley Temple and every boy Clark Gable.

Reindeer in the Frylics of 1935. *From left to right, front row*: Ann Page Brock, Carol Jones, Alice Subley and Terry Epstein. *Back row*: Betty Jane Terrell and Ernestine Allport. *Courtesy of Bettie Terrell Hobson and the Whitaker Studio.*

A party tradition had students coming up one at a time to sing a carol with Miss Fry and choosing the carol. Mary Rolfe O'Neill Joyner vividly recalled singing "Silent Night" with Miss Fry each year. If a child was shy, he or she didn't have to participate or could go up with a friend.

Adults were relegated to the balcony while the children partied and got a visit from Santa. Miss Fry gave each child a small gift, some of which are fondly recalled to this day. It wasn't just a ring or a pin; it was a personal gift from Miss Fry, the person you idolized and worshipped as much as, or in some cases more than, anyone in the world. Winifred Slater Hazelton will never forget the "pearl" bracelet with tiny "gold" ballet slippers and Page Hobson Bourgeois fondly recalls a sterling silver charm bracelet she received with her name engraved on one side and "Frylics of 1964" on the other. Many dancers recall receiving a Kennedy silver half dollar on a chain. The assistants received pieces of silver for their sterling silver place settings, which for many of them came at the time when they were first starting their collections. The students often pooled their money to buy one gift for Miss Fry.

In the weeks leading up to the party, Miss Fry taught students the waltz and fox trot, which they performed at the party.

The two-person donkey costume was often pulled out for the party and turned into Rudolf. Used regularly in the Frylics, the costume could be a donkey, a zebra, a reindeer or whatever four-legged creature was needed for a particular dance. Decades later, Mary Rolfe O'Neill Joyner happily recalled being the rear end and Marie Jones being the front. Another tradition had all the kids line up, holding hands. They would form a circle, getting tighter and tighter until the beginning and end of the line met. Since the first and last person in line got to hold hands with Miss Fry, everyone wanted to be first or last.

When former pupils reminisce about their time with Miss Fry, they happily go back to the Christmas parties—laughing, singing and loads of entertainment. As one dancer gleefully recalled, "We all felt so special and grown up in our party finery. Music, dancing, balloons, poppers, ice cream, cakes, candy—what a party! What a bash!"

IV
DANCE THEMES

Miss Fry's dance numbers dealt with various themes and topics—funny, educational, clever and sometimes downright silly. For the pupils and the parents, the recitals were electrifying, perhaps the most exciting day of the year. Parents wouldn't think of not attending both matinee and evening recitals. Miss Fry always did the butterfly or swan dance, either at the end of Act I or to start Act 2, to allow her time to get in position to conduct the show.

Mothers could go to the ballroom before the recitals to help get their children ready. A few mothers, along with the assistants, escorted the children backstage. For the rehearsals and recitals, students lined up—holding hands—in a long line that snaked through the back hallway to the backstage area, so the students in the number that came up next were ready to go on stage immediately after the number before them ended. With hundreds of students in forty or fifty different numbers in a single recital, you can imagine that long line of enthusiastic kids, from three to eighteen years of age, waiting to go on stage. It's no wonder Edith Lindeman was so impressed with the crispness of the shows. Roger Riggle Jr., who has made a career in dance, still marvels at the creativity and logistical skill of having so many students perform. He compared the recitals to Christmas Spectaculars at Radio City Music Hall.

The 1950 Frylics featured Nancy Jones as an old-fashioned schoolteacher doing a novelty tap number while standing on her hands. Marion Mease Childrey starred as "Flame" in an Evolution of Light number; Bettie Jane

"Swan Dance"—perhaps Miss Fry's personal favorite. *Courtesy of the Valentine Richmond History Center.*

Terrell was featured in "Lady of the Evening"; and thirteen girls performed "Girls on the Pink Police Gazette." Harriet Leah Salsbury and Cheryl Ahern performed in 1956's "Betty Crocker's Devil's Food Cake."

There were big-picture themes, too, like doing good and accepting different people and different cultures. Linda Fiske Wehrle happily remembers the performances at the Veterans' Hospital. She later became a nurse in the U.S. Navy during the Vietnam War and believes learning about muscles and how the body moved through dance helped her in orthopedic surgery. In addition, values emphasized in the dance lessons like discipline, patience and working with others helped, too. Miss Fry would have been exceptionally proud of her students, especially when they were doing good—like volunteering to help others.

One theme that came up several times involved children on one side of the stage skipping to the other side, with one child eventually following them. But before the stray girl could join her peers, the group skipped to the opposite side, rejecting her. This was repeated several times. Finally, the odd girl out, saddened, went to the center of the stage and put her hands over her eyes as if crying. Realizing the hurt they caused, the group ran to the middle and formed a circle around the lone girl, and they all skipped off happily together. This theme was repeated several times, including in "Little Guilty

"Polka Dots" in the Frylics of 1940. *From left to right:* Jeans Mays, Marietta Chandler, Nancy Lee Archbell, Grace Bloxsom and Jeanne Jenkins. *Courtesy of Nancy Lee Archbell Bain. Photo taken by Whitaker Studio.*

Conscience." During a 1946 number with cute little lambs, the girls dressed in white fuzzy leotards; the outsider stood alone in a black fuzzy leotard. At the end of the routine, they happily coalesced and skipped off together. Accept others. Don't be mean. Life lessons learned through dance.

TOPICAL AND FADS

In 1934, the iconic Blue Eagle of the National Recovery Act (NRA) was everywhere, tucked away somewhere in the corners of signs and advertisements. Its ubiquity unmistakable, even the NFL football team from Philadelphia was named for it. Years later, the team changed it from a blue eagle to a green one. At the same time, gold also became a topical point of interest because it became illegal for private citizens to possess gold; with few exceptions, people were required to sell their gold to the federal government. So the 1934 Frylics had several numbers related to the NRA Blue Eagle and gold. "We're in the Money" showed dancers in the "Gold Standard" and the "Silver Standard." Almost eight decades later, Patsy Garrett vividly recalls being the gold, dressed in gold-colored leotards and carrying gold money. Marion Mease did a toe solo in "Under the Blue Eagle." When recycled in the 1961 Frylics, Eileen Lawlor played the NRA Blue Eagle.

Shirley Temple was the popular child movie star of the late 1930s, and several Frylics brought Shirley Temple lookalikes into various routines. Three decades later, in 1963, Adair Lee Branner played the Shirley Temple doll. Several former dancers remarked that all the girls wanted to be Shirley Temple.

Brother Rat, a movie about cadets at the Virginia Military Institute starring Ronald Reagan and Jane Wyman, was released in 1938. It wasn't long before the Frylics had a number impersonating *Brother Rats*. Shortly after the Cavalier Arena opened, Miss Fry assembled a roller-skating number. Bette Bloxsom Witherington remembers this particularly well because her mother and Jody Weaver's mother were among the skaters. Bette and her sister Grace were greatly relieved when the curtain fell to end that number and their mother was still standing—or at least rolling. Miss Fry's pupils ("Miss Elinor Fry's Skating Lassies," an advertisement called them)[71] performed several times at the Cavalier ("Air Conditioned!"), including the June 1942 party to celebrate the arena's first anniversary.

Miss Fry cobbled together dances in the 1960s to match the popular musicals of the decade—*My Fair Lady* (1964), *Mary Poppins* (1964) and *The*

Sound of Music (1965). The Frylics of 1964 included *The Fairest of the Fair*, with dance numbers such as "Cotton Candy," "Popcorn," "Candy Apples," "Balloons," "Ring Master," "Circus Ponies," "Magician" (in which the magician, David Allan Schneider, pulled the bunny, Terry Dorsey Dalton, out of an oversized hat) and "Fair Restaurant." The "Fair Restaurant" dance spun off several more numbers: "Coffee," "Lettuce," "Tomatoes,"

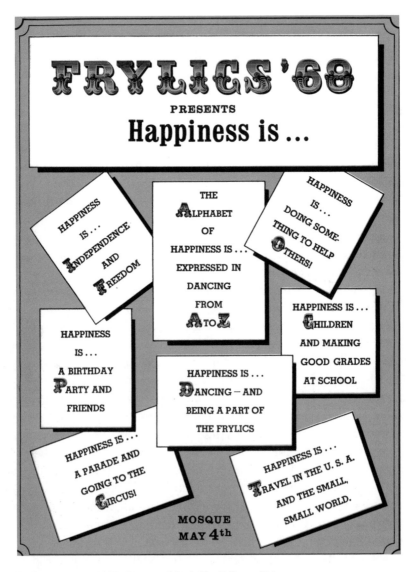

Frylics program, 1968. *Courtesy of Bettie Terrell Dorsey Hobson.*

"Waiters," "Cherry Tarts" and "Candy & Cake." Titled *Music the Whole World Loves*, the 1966 Frylics included songs and dance numbers for *My Fair Lady*, *Mary Poppins* ("Jolly Holiday," "A Spoonful of Sugar") and *The Sound of Music* ("So Long, Farewell," "Lonely Goat Herd," "My Favorite Things" and "Edelweiss").

The Frylics of 1967 included "I Dream of Jeannie" and "The Mod Look," depicting the popular television show of the era and the fashion zeitgeist.

Music was also represented. "The Girl Watcher's Song," "The Third Man Theme" and "Shake, Rattle and Roll" were introduced as dances right after these musical tunes became popular. Mickey Garrett sang "King of the Road" in the 1966 show, and after *Butch Cassidy and the Sundance Kid* made it to the theaters, "Raindrops Keep Falling on My Head"—the popular song from the movie—made it into the Frylics, sung by Roger Riggle Jr. and his sister, Amy, who were frequently paired to sing together in many Frylics. Some of their other songs included "Tell Me Pretty Maiden," "It's a Small, Small World" and "The Right Somebody to Love."

After Disneyland opened, the Frylics included a "Mouseketeers" number. Famous Walt Disney characters were not left out. Children danced as "Snow White," "Mickey Mouse," "Donald Duck" and "Tinker Bell" (played by Anne Reynolds). In the 1968 show, one act contained dances for each letter of the alphabet, with "Disneyland" getting the *d*.

At the end of the decade, with cultural and pop references of peace, love, flowers and things "psychedelic," the 1969 Frylics incorporated dances called "Love Beads," "Psychedelic Flowers," "Psychedelic Prints" and "Doves of Peace." The 1969 Frylics, with the theme *Love Makes the World Go Round*, included an act with famous couples from history, such as Cleopatra and Mark Anthony

Nancy Lee Archbell at three years, ten months old. The groom was Billie McKemmie. Frylics of 1939. *Courtesy of Nancy Lee Archbell Bain.*

(played by Betty Bradley Jones and Cindy Sharp), Romeo and Juliet (Hazel Rippe and Cindy Sharp) and Josephine and Napoleon (Jana Privette and Kevin Stewart Broom). Weddings were always big. In the 1952 Frylics, Gale Hutzler played the Flower Girl in the "Wedding" of Bettie Jane Terrell (bride) and Mary Clay Atkinson (groom).

Nancy Lee Archbell Bain recalls marrying Billie McKemmie in "Wedding of the Kewpie Dolls." At the time, she was three years old. She still has a great framed photograph of the dance with ten bridesmaids and nine flower girls.

Snow White and the Seven Dwarfs was released in 1937, so soon afterward the Frylics impersonated the movie's characters. Dorothy Farley got to be Dopey, Raymond Wright was Prince Charming and Patsy Garrett played Snow White.

GYPSIES, SPORTS, PERFUMES AND CARDS

La Verne Lupton performed as a gypsy acrobat in the 1934 Frylics, and the 1949 show had a "Gypsy Moon" number. The 1938 Frylics finished with "Gypsies," as did the 1970 show (Darlene Bagby in this final number); another recital highlighted a "pseudo-televised visit to the land of gypsies."[72] W.D. Hasty Jr. sang the "Gypsy Love Song." Hasty sang many songs in various Frylics, including "Give My Regards to Broadway," "This Is My Country" and "Standing on the Corner." Like most themes, the gypsy dance could be traced back to Miss Fry's childhood. In this case, in the spring of 1916, twelve-year-old Miss Fry did a gypsy dance for a garden party at the Masonic Temple.

"Highlights in the World of Sport" included a fencing number. Miss Fry had done some fencing over the years and took lessons in Europe in 1934. The 1937 show included "A Baseball Nine," with each of the ballplayers throwing a baseball (actually, a tennis ball, according to Skippy Ford, one of the performers) into the audience. Mrs. Hobson later got one of the balls back and gave it to her brother Billy, who had performed in the number. "Highlights in the World of Sports" also included separate dances for "Skaters," "Golf," "Tennis," "Fencing" and—featuring the four Lange sisters and the four Lewis sisters—"A Hunting We Will Go." The Frylics of 1959 included dances for "Parker Field" and "Baseball Fans."

The Frylics illustrated a perfume department and dances for "Piquant [*sic*] Perfume," "Evening in Paris," "Cupid's Breath" (performed by a group of three-year-olds), "Soul of the Violet," "Miracle Perfume" (enlightened by strobe lights) and "Gardenias" (girls in green dresses with white gardenias). A line of gardenias fronted the stage at the Mosque for the Frylics shows. To this day, sixty years later, Wade Ogg thinks of Miss Fry and the Frylics whenever he smells gardenias.

Miss Fry was big on hearts. Hearts—the playing card variety—along with diamonds, spades and clubs played a significant role. Spectators at the 1938 Frylics saw an entire "Deck of Cards"—fifty-three dancers, each dressed as a card. The hearts and diamonds wore vivid red, gold and white, while the spades wore black, gold and white. Charles Gilbert Henley played the joker. There were also numbers called "Spades and Hearts," "Diamonds and Clubs," "Jacks," "Queens," "Kings" and "Aces." The playing card number came back in subsequent shows, including the 1970 show, when it was called "Game Time." Many of the longtime dancers and instructors danced in "Spades and Hearts".

POLKAS, BOOGIES, WALTZES AND MISS AMERICAS

Miss Fry peppered her shows with polkas, and it makes perfect sense when you realize one of the first times her name was printed in the newspaper—in April 1910—the six-year-old was dancing the "Kindergarten Polka" at the Jefferson Hotel during the Mother Goose Carnival.[73] After that, how could polkas not become a regular staple?

Theatergoers over the years would have seen Miss Fry's dancers perform the "Hop Scotch Polka," "Sicilian Polka," "Viennese Polka," "Pennsylvania Polka" and even the "Swiss Polka." Perhaps the most creative polka of all, however, was 1941's "Firefly Ballet," which consisted of twenty-one girls impersonating fireflies, tiny electric lights concealed beneath their wings. Somehow, Miss Fry snuck in a polka, too.

If you have polkas, you certainly need boogies and waltzes. Ireland, for example, was represented in various Frylics with the "Irish Boogie." All kinds of waltzes were demonstrated over the years, including the "Easter Waltz," "Sweetheart Waltz," "Rock and Roll Waltz," "Old-Fashioned Waltz," "Skaters Waltz," "Dutch Waltzes" (in wooden shoes of course), "Firefly Waltz," "Waltz Rhythm Tap," "Waltz of the Flowers," of course the "Tennessee Waltz," the "Merry Widow Waltz" and even something called the "Waltzing Cat," featuring Jane Cleveland Thomas.

Above: "Waltz of the Flowers":
Linda Salsbury (left), Barney
Chiddick (center, standing), Ruth
Ann King (center, floor) and Ann
Galloway (right). *Courtesy of Linda
Salsbury Weinstein; photo taken by
Adolph Rice Studio.*

Left: "Merry Widow Waltz":
Linda Salsbury and Joseph
Edward Parker Jr. Frylics of 1950.
*Courtesy of Linda Salsbury Weinstein;
photo taken by Wedgewood Studio.*

Another recurring theme—usually introduced in dance numbers about Atlantic City or the state of New Jersey—was future Miss America contests. The 1951 Frylics had a dance called "Miss Americas of 1965," the 1959 Frylics included "Miss Americas of 1975" and the 1968 Frylics revealed "Miss Americas of 1985," which at the time must have seemed out of this world. Futuristic beauty queens aside, celestial and galaxy themes came up frequently.

Moon, Planets, Stars and Galaxy

The galaxy provided a regular source of amusement. The first number of the first Frylics (of 1933), "Moonlight and Roses," got repeated many times in subsequent Frylics. The 1939 show began with *The Ballet of the Stars and Planets*, which included separate dances called "Milky Way," "Twinkle Twinkle Little Star," "Saturn and Its Rings," "The Evening Star" and "The Venus Ballet." *The Mercury Ballet* started with five dancers and a large silk square dotted with luminous stars and closed with a flawless precision tap of the planets. "Mars" was represented with four girls wearing costumes of silver jewel cloth, with red flowing capes and silver helmets.

Miss Fry often sent cards to her pupils, handwritten and replete with colorful drawings. One such card shows stars and hearts, raindrops, flowers, the sun and the moon. Around those little drawings, she wrote:

> *Happiness is—in every heart and will be shared if we do our part—for it takes the summer sun and rain to make a garden grow—it takes the moon and twinkling stars to make the heavens glow—it takes lots of practice and hard work to make a dream come true—so set your goal when you decide what happiness is—for you! With Love—Miss Fry.*[74]

Planetarium in the 1956 show included "When You Wish Upon a Star," "Moonbeam" and "Venus." The theme for the 1948 recital was *Heaven and Earth*, and the 1958 show featured *Stars and Moonlight*, with children impersonating "Baby Moons" and "Ring Around Saturn." The 1962 astronaut-themed show—*Out of This World*—included "Lucky Stars," "Twinkling Stars," "Star Dust," "Hitch Your Wagon to a Star," "Astronaut and Family" and "Outer Space." The program cover featured a drawing

To bring this poetry thing to pass —
was my one great ambition —
But to bring that many gifts I couldn't
get the U. S. Customs permission
and then too — it was far beyond my
financial condition!

So —

I'm sending this little picture of me in my
Swan Costume to you, my Dear
As a small memento of this "My swan song year"
and I hope it will serve as —
"Something to Remember me by"
with the love and admiration of your
Devoted Teacher — Elinor Fry.

Card to students with gift boxes. Miss Fry often sent personal cards to her students. *Courtesy of Bettie Terrell Dorsey Hobson.*

Frylics program, 1962. *Courtesy of Bettie Terrell Dorsey Hobson.*

of two kids riding a rocket. Among other sisters dancing in the 1962 show were the Privettes (Jana, Pamela and Renee), and the Goldbergs (Jacqueline, Linda and Laura).

Miss Fry's shows were indeed topical. Whatever was new and popular at the time often made its way into dance routines.

COLONIAL MINUETS AND DRESS BALLS

In February 1928, Miss Fry and her advanced pupils performed for the George Washington Ball, with a minuet featuring fifty young dancers dressed in colonial costumes.

Colonial minuet dance—a regular staple of many Frylics. *Courtesy of Marjorie Branner Adams.*

In October 1928, they performed their signature minuet dance in colonial costumes at a star-studded event for Virginia governor Harry Byrd, Senator Swanson, five former Virginia governors and Lady Astor (Richmond's own

Nancy Langhorne) at the Governor's Ball (the first in Richmond since colonial days). Two members of the Richmond Light Infantry Blues, dressed in white-plumed helmets and dark blue uniforms, brought in a huge basket covered in ribbons and roses. Released from the basket, Miss Fry—in a gleaming white satin dress, trimmed attractively with silver lace and rhinestone—did

Miss Fry at the Governor's Ball, October 1928. *Courtesy of the Valentine Richmond History Center.*

a solo graceful toe dance as the feature of the ball. When she finished, she presented each of the ladies in the official party with a bouquet from the basket. Two days later, the minuet dancers traveled to Charlottesville, where they performed at Monticello, with photographs of them making it into the April 1929 *National Geographic*.

They were back again in colonial garb in January 1931's Confederate Ball at the John Marshall Hotel and in November 1932 at the Jefferson Hotel. The April 1937 *National Geographic* included photographs of Miss Fry and some of her pupils from an event in Williamsburg, Virginia.

On April 13, 1910, when she was six years old, Miss Fry performed at a fancy dress ball at Belvidere Hall. In February 1924, the papers reported that Miss Fry and her mother were returning from the Virginia Military Institute's Fancy Dress Ball. Each year in the late 1920s, a notice appeared in late January about Miss Fry performing at the Washington and Lee University Fancy Dress Ball. In 1928, she and four of her star students (Emily Thompson, Mary Todd, Mary Griffith and Anita Wyland) danced "In the Storm" at the ball. Shortly afterward, the event's director sent a thank-you letter: "I have seen interpretive dances both here and abroad and I am frank when I say that it was one of the finest I have ever seen."[75] In the 1929 ball (theme: Arabian Nights), Miss Fry danced "Tale of the Dancing Girl" and "Dance Oriental." Years later, many Frylics incorporated dances honoring these balls, such as "Washington and Lee Fancy Dress Ball" and "Washington and Lee Swing."

Tobacco, Parades, Drill and Military

Dressed like little soldiers, with uniforms and wooden play rifles, dancers marching in drill formation were regular features of recitals, charity events and the annual Tobacco Festivals, which took place in Richmond each fall from 1949 to 1984. With its own float, the Elinor Fry School of Dance marched in the parades, ending at Parker Field. A performance at the Jefferson Hotel or the John Marshall often culminated the festivities, during a ball where one of the tobacco princesses from around the state was crowned Queen of Tobaccoland.

Miss Fry's pupils performed a half-hour "Patriotic Fantasia" and a drill at halftime shows of football games during the festival. The Tobacco Festival included a performance of *Tobaccorama* ("the story of tobacco in song and dance")[76] at the Mosque. Former pupils recall the excitement of marching in the drill, where the youngest dancers got to dance with the "big girls"; that is, the seventeen- and eighteen-year-olds. When Miss Fry brought in Cornelia Connell—a former Rockette—as an instructor in the late 1950s, the tempo turned the drill more into a Rockettes theme. Dancers in the drill had to be able to high-kick five feet.

Bettie Jane Terrell, "The Lady in Red," Frylics of 1953.

To learn how to march and carry play rifles, real United States Marine drill instructors trained the dancers (in Richmond and Quantico). The dancers' costumes at the halftime shows consisted of short satin blue skirts (red underneath), white belts, dark blue short jackets, hats resembling those of marines, gold buttons and wooden play rifles. When they performed the drill on the field, real marines (in dress uniforms) were right there, too.

There was often a drill in the recitals, creatively demonstrated with different names and themes. One drill consisted of seventy-six trombones in a big parade with, of course, seventy-six children. To shake things up, other drills featured seventy-six children playing kazoos and something called the "Flirtation Walk."

Two of Miss Fry's former students were selected in the 1930s as "Cigarette Girls" for promotional campaigns of well-known brands. In Richmond, Marion Mease became the Domino Cigarette Girl when she was twelve years old, and a few years later, Patsy Garrett became the Chesterfield Girl in New York. Garrett told me she and Marion had a good laugh about each of them becoming "famous" cigarette girls. For the 1940 Frylics, Patsy Garrett returned to Richmond to sing, "When a Cigarette Is Burning," the theme song of her nightly radio broadcast at the time.

In a number about the States in the 1951 Frylics, Richmond was represented in the Virginia act as the world's largest cigarette manufacturing center. The 1959 show included *Tobacco Row*, with separate dances for "American Tobacco Company," "Lucky Strike," "Call for Phillip Morris," "Kools," "Domino Cigarettes," "Smoke Gets in Your Eyes," "Vice Roy [*sic*]," "Chesterfield," "Encore Filter Cigarettes," "L&Ms" and "Herbert Tareyton." Chesterfield cigarettes were advertised on the back cover of Frylics' programs from 1935 to 1941, before that space was taken over for advertisements promoting Richmond hotels.

The military was well represented in dance routines. Miss Fry's scrapbooks are replete with letters of thanks and commendations from military units, including McGuire Veterans' Hospital, Fort Lee and the U.S. Marine Corps Recruiting Service. Mrs. Hobson recalls that she, Fay Long Lovering and Nancy Barker Jones dressed up as cigarette girls, dancing on Sunday nights at the McGuire Hospital Auditorium. After the dance, they handed out cigarettes.

For many years, the advanced students performed a mini-recital a week after the annual Frylics for the veterans at McGuire's Hospital. You can imagine how gratifying it must have been for the old soldiers.

Ed Adams was stationed at Fort Lee at the time. Hearing about Miss Fry's dancing girls—all five hundred of them—prompted him and his buddies to

Cigarette girls, circa World War II. *From left to right*: Bettie Jane Terrell, Fay Long and Nancy Barker. *Courtesy of Bettie Terrell Dorsey Hobson.*

hop in the car and drive to Richmond to check them out. Unfortunately for the eager soldiers, no one had told them the ages of the dancers.

According to a mid-1950s newspaper article, Miss Fry's students did about twenty to twenty-five exhibitions annually at military posts, performing

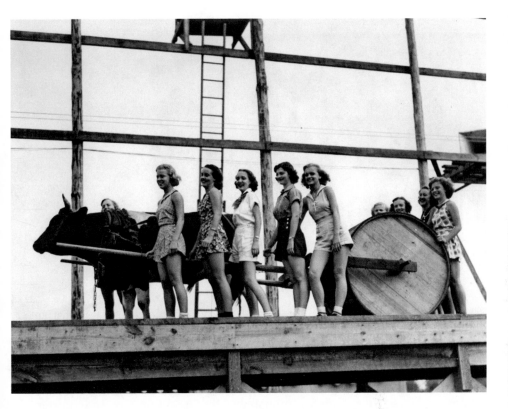

The 1937 Richmond Bicentennial. *Courtesy of Bettie Terrell Dorsey Hobson.*

pretty much wherever and whenever there was "a need and request for fresh, young faces and spirited pretty dancing."[77] One photo from the scrapbook shows several dancers on stage with a bull.

The 1953 Frylics included a drill with forty-two dancers. Other 1950s numbers included "Tell It to the Marines" (Anne Cannon in this), "Parris Island," "K.P. Duty," "Target Practice" and "Rifle Drill." The 1957 show ended with "Iwo Jima."

The American Legion and the American Legion Ladies' Auxiliary sponsored the shows during World War II (and all subsequent years) when Miss Fry's troupe—the "Bond-a-Liers"—mobilized their efforts to sell war bonds.

Newspapers of the day reported performances at an array of venues. A May 1942 show, benefiting the Soldiers' Emergency Relief Fund, concluded with a finale of 40 girls (as young as three) twirling batons. Other bond shows included the "Okay America Revue" and the "Personality Party," with 4,700 in attendance.[78] Patsy Garrett also performed at the Personality Party.

Miss Fry and Ellis Schwab receiving an award for raising money for war bonds. *Courtesy of Bettie Terrell Dorsey Hobson.*

The Bond-a-Liers rolled through various Virginia locales. A road trip in June 1944 to Tappahannock netted $32,775 in bond sales. On the late-night bus ride home after the performance, the happy dancers gave boisterous cheers, including one for their own Ellis Schwab, who, in addition to performing in the show, also worked nights at the post office. Schwab was unusually old for the Frylics, probably in his late twenties or early thirties when he participated in the shows. Taking note of these efforts, the United States Treasury publicly thanked Miss Fry and her dancers.

Several shows included patriotic themes, such as *Victory Garden*, with dancers impersonating "Farmers," "Lettuce," "Tomatoes," "Corn" and "Carrots." The scarecrow, played by Ellis Schwab, suddenly came to life, according to Edith Lindeman, "after fifteen minutes of almost unbelievable immobility."[79] The finale that year: "The Victory Polka."

The 1942 show included a dance for each month of the year. "December" was represented, not with a Christmas theme, but rather by a patriotic one, with Jody Weaver and Bette Bloxsom singing "Remember Pearl Harbor." Bette recalls being held offstage, unable to join her friend Jody in the tap line because a very conscientious stagehand mistakenly held her back. No matter how much she persisted, the stagehand was unrelenting. But not to worry. The orchestra played the intro again, Miss Fry smiled and waved her on and, finally, one of the assistants convinced the stagehand that Bette was indeed supposed to be on stage. With four or five kids performing in about fifty different numbers, it's a wonder there weren't issues like this dozens of times in each recital.

V
FRYLICS

L isted here are the themes for the Frylics. There were no Frylics for the years 1943 through 1946. The program covers before 1942 did not have a single theme.

1942: Around the Calendar
1947: A Modern Department Store
1948: Heaven and Earth
1949: Present, Past and Future
1950: Frylics of Fifty
1951: Our United States
1952: Dancing Through Life
1953: Say It with Flowers
1954: On with the Dance
1955: Hit Parade
1956: Leisure and Pleasure
1957: Songs of the Islands
1958: Melody of the Bells
1959: A Book Revue of Virginia
1960: Greetings and Best Wishes
1961: 25th Anniversary Recital
1962: Out of This World
1963: Collectors' Items
1964: The Fairest of the Fair

1965: Out of the Magazine Rack
1966: Music the Whole World Loves
1967: Good News
1968: Happiness Is
1969: Love Makes the World Go Round
1970: Moments to Remember

A routine could be about the months of the year, like 1942's "Around the Calendar." January revealed numbers for each of the following: "The Skaters," "Penguins," "Snow Flakes," "Reindeer" and "Snowballs." February: "Does Your Heart Beat for Me?" "Humpty Dumpty Heart," "Old-Fashioned Valentines" and "Valentina"; March: "March Winds," "Irish Eyes," "Rose O'Day" and "Spring Time"; and April: "In Your Easter Bonnet," "Easter Chicks," "Easter Bunnies," "April Showers," "Extase" and "Lilacs."

Taking it directly from an Edith Lindeman review:

> *January was ushered in by wee Annette Butler. February was characterized by Valentines dances, comic and otherwise, with a delightful "Minuet on Toe" by Dolores Curry...March brought winds with their batik scarves... tiny Nancy Lee Archbell was a big hit as "Spring." Bunnies jumped up and down, and showers brought little girls with flower-sprinkled parasols in April. June was a conglomeration of roses, graduates, brides, grooms, and beach girls. August opened with a beautiful flamingo ballet, and September brought school days in which Dorothy Farley drew pictures and danced on the same huge slate. October was accepted with phosphorescent pumpkins, a Halloween novelty, which featured dancing skeletons against a dead black background, and a fine acrobatic number, "Indian Summer," danced by Marian Mease...November brought all the leaves and flowers of autumn.*[80]

The theme could simply be, as in 1947, *A Modern Department Store*, with the things you'd see in one, such as the "Men's Department," "Jewelry Department," "Perfume Counter," "Record Shop," "Bride's Shop" and the "Toy Department," which spun off "Dancing Dolls," "Ballet Dolls," "Kewpie Dolls," "Toy Bunnies," "Majorette Dolls," "Story Book Dolls," "Peter Pan Dolls," "Gingham Dogs and Calico Cats" and "Wooden Soldiers."

The "Bride's Shop" featured six sets of sisters: the Shafers, Trevillians, Marrins, McDonnells, Wolfes and Hulls, an impressive sister accomplishment on par with the 1939 Frylics, which featured the four Lange sisters (Mary,

Bumblebees: Betty Slater (middle), Cheryl Pierce (to the right of Betty as you look at the picture), Joan Marks (bottom right) and Linda Salsbury (far right, standing). *Courtesy of Linda Salsbury Weinstein.*

Katherine Anne, Marguerite and Thelma), the four Lewises (Mary Katherine, Dorothy, Eleanor and Margaret), the three Beckhs (Jacqueline, Hilda and Jean) and the David twins (Barbara and Marion) performing together in a single dance.

The 1949 show *Present, Past and Future* revealed days of the week: "Wash on Monday," "Iron on Tuesday," "Sweep on Wednesday," "Mend on Thursday" (fourteen girls were dressed as thread, another fourteen as pin cushions, and Marion Mease did a specialty number dressed as a pair of scissors), "Scrub on Friday" (Nancy Jones, according to a newspaper review, made a hit as the scrub woman), "Bake on Saturday" and "Church on Sunday" (featuring Carol Norman singing "Ava Maria").

There were plenty of old-fashioned song and dance numbers. The 1939 recital opened with ten little girls, four- and five-year-olds, playing chopsticks on toy pianos. Hopefully somewhere, someone has a good picture of this. If I could have found such a photograph, it would be in this book. The 1950 recital, *Frylics of Fifty*, highlighted music of the first half of the twentieth

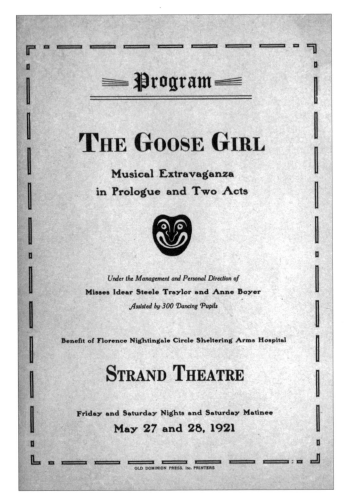

=== Program ===

THE GOOSE GIRL

Musical Extravaganza
in Prologue and Two Acts

Under the Management and Personal Direction of
Misses Idear Steele Traylor and Anne Boyer
Assisted by 300 Dancing Pupils

Benefit of Florence Nightingale Circle Sheltering Arms Hospital

STRAND THEATRE

Friday and Saturday Nights and Saturday Matinee
May 27 and 28, 1921

OLD DOMINION PRESS. Inc. PRINTERS

"The Goose Girl," 1921. Miss Elinor Fry was the star pupil of the Tray-Boy dance studio, established by Idear Steele Traylor and Anne Boyer. Tray-Boy put on its first annual recital in 1918. *Courtesy of the author.*

century: "Bessie in a Bustle" ("little girls in lavender taffeta costumes with bustles on the back almost as large as the dancers, who range from less than a yard tall to three feet, three inches"),[81] "Gibson Girls," "Pony Boy," "Yama Yama Girls," "Oh You Beautiful Doll," "Pretty Baby," "Meet Me Tonight in Dreamland" and "The Floradora Sextette," which might have caused Miss Fry's mind to wander back to 1921, when she danced the same number in that year's Tray-Boy "Goose Girl" production. Floradora was the name of a popular turn-of-the-century musical.

The 1966 Frylics, *Music the Whole World Loves*, included songs from the Roaring Twenties ("Charleston," "Sweet Georgia Brown" and "St. Louis Blues") and tunes by Victor Herbert, including, of course, "Toyland" (sung

Miss Fry began dancing at a young age and never stopped. *Courtesy of the Valentine Richmond History Center.*

Bettie Terrell in "Pipes of Pan," circa 1935. *Courtesy of Bettie Terrell Dorsey Hobson.*

GREEN SATIN

gold
sequin
NOTES.

YELLOW
RUFFLES UNDER
NEATH EDGED
gold ribbon.

(front of
costume)

Suggestion —

use music —
" Fit as a fiddle "

(Back of
costume)

" Fit as a fiddle."

Costume drawings—"Fit as
a Fiddle." Miss Fry designed
each costume. Each recital
included thousands of hand-
sewn costumes. *Courtesy of
Bettie Terrell Dorsey Hobson.*

Right: Amy Riggle and Roger Riggle Jr. The versatile duo sang many tunes in the Frylics, including "Toyland," "Raindrops Keep Falling on My Head" and "It's a Small, Small World." *Courtesy of Roger Riggle Jr.*

Below: Goldberg sisters, circa 1962. *From left to right*: Jacqueline Diane, Linda Lisa and Laura Jeanne. *Courtesy of Jacqueline Jones.*

Miss Fry, married in September 1941 to Stuart Wesley Phillips. After the wedding, the newlyweds made a motor trip to Maine. *Courtesy of the Valentine Richmond History Center.*

Linda Lisa Goldberg, Frylics of 1965. *Courtesy of Jacqueline Jones.*

Painting of Miss Fry, circa 1941. Artist unknown. *Courtesy of de Veaux Riddick.*

Frylics program, 1933. Helen Keller attended the first Frylics. Her speech went on so long that many of the dancers did not get a chance to perform on stage. *Courtesy of Bettie Terrell Dorsey Hobson.*

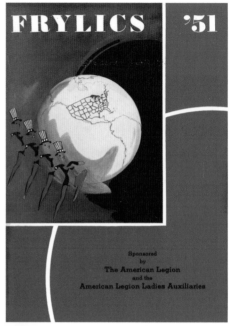

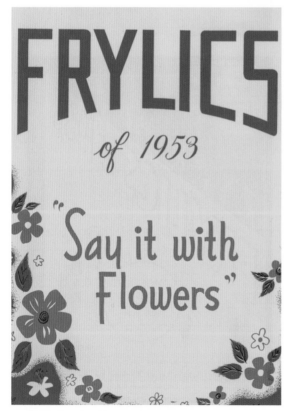

Above, left: Frylics program, 1949.
Courtesy of Bettie Terrell Dorsey Hobson.

Above, right: Frylics program, 1951.
Courtesy of Bettie Terrell Dorsey Hobson.

Left: Frylics program, 1953. *Courtesy of Bettie Terrell Dorsey Hobson.*

Frylics program, 1957. *Courtesy of Bettie Terrell Dorsey Hobson.*

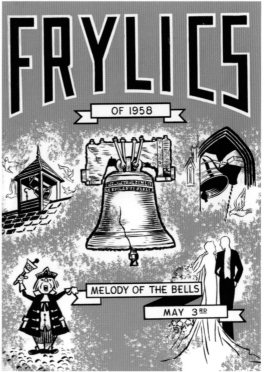

Frylics program, 1958. *Courtesy of Bettie Terrell Dorsey Hobson.*

Frylics program, 1959. *Courtesy of Bettie Terrell Dorsey Hobson.*

Frylics program, 1964. *Courtesy of Bettie Terrell Dorsey Hobson.*

by Amy Riggle and Roger Riggle Jr.). The "Good Ship Lollipop" and "Polly Wolly Doodle"—songs made famous in Shirley Temple movies—were included in several recitals.

States were presented over the years. The 1951 show, *Our United States*, was devoted to all forty-eight of them, plus the territories of Alaska and Hawaii and many cities. Wayne Johnson played Uncle Sam. The "New Orleans Mardi Gras Festival" was depicted by girls dressed in cerise (French for cherry) colored satin, trimmed with bright balls of gold; for Kentucky, six girls costumed as ponies and six as jockeys danced the "Kentucky Derby." Maryland was revealed with fourteen children dressed as "Orioles," and California got the "Pasadena Tournament of Roses." The "Pennsylvania Polka" depicted the Keystone State, the "St. Louis Blues" the Show Me State and the "Tennessee Waltz" the Volunteer State. Oklahoma had an "Indian Pow Wow" starring Grace Bloxsom, with Julia Browder (as the chief) doing an acrobatic solo. The North Star State (Minnesota) revealed six girls dancing "You Are My Lucky Star." Florida got several dances: "Way Down upon the Swanee River," "Fountain of Youth," "On Miami Shores," "Tallahassee" and "Moon over Miami," an acrobatic number with beach balls. Richmond was honored with a salute to the "Apple Blossom

"Rose Trellises," Frylics of 1959. *Courtesy of Debbie Markel, photo by Adolph Rice Studio.*

Festival." Mallie Theimer, a junior at Wilson High School in Portsmouth, performed as drum majorette for the drill. She had recently, according to a news account, exhibited her baton twirling skills throughout Virginia and adjacent territories. In the next year's "Dancing Dolls" routine, Jo Ann Ahern was featured as the majorette.

The show could render famous quotations and familiar old sayings, like 1954's *On with the Dance*. With a literary nod, the program opened with a quote from Lord Byron's poem, "The Eve of Waterloo": "On with the dance. Let joy be unconfin'd. No sleep till morn, when youth and pleasure meet to chase the glowing hours with flying feet." Common expressions, and some not so common, made it into the show as dances, including "Make It Snappy," "Let Freedom Ring," "Going Around in Circles," "Variety Is the Spice of Life," "Children Should Be Seen and not Heard," "A Chip Off the Old Block," "As Busy as a Bee," "As Sweet as Honey," "Happy as a Lark," "Knee Deep in Clover," "When the Cat's Away the Mice Will Play" (with "The Cat's Meow" and "As Quiet as a Mouse"), "It Never Rains—But It Pours," "Tell It to the Marines," "On with the Dance," "Twinkle Twinkle Little Star," "Belle of the Ball," "One Picture Is Worth a Thousand Words," "Too Many Cooks Spoil the Broth," "Fit for a King" (Joey Smith was king), "Roses Are Red," "As Fresh as a Daisy" (includes: "Daises Won't Tell" and "Daisy Chain"), "He Loves Me—He Loves Me Not," "All That Glitters Is Not Gold," "Stop, Look and Listen," "Stick to Your Guns," "Better Late Than Never," "Vaya Con Dios" (Pamela Fry was in this—no relation to Miss Fry) and the finale, "All's Well That Ends Well." Also in this show were "Bulls" (with James Galloway and Larry Bambacus) and "Time and Tide Wait for No Man" (danced by Miss Fry).

In two recitals (1955 and 1961), Miss Fry pulled together dances from each of the prior Frylics. The leadoff numbers in 1955 and 1961 were the same as the first one from 1933: "Moonlight and Roses." The 1955 show also featured "Pickett Fences" (the girls lay on their backs and raised their legs— the pickets—in the air) and the Hawaiian number "Little Hula Hands":

Little hula hands so graceful
Learn to dance like mommy can
Make the moon above, shining on the land
Make the gentle rain, falling on the sand

Little hula hands so graceful
Throw a kiss to someone you love

"Pipes of Pan." *From left to right, back row:* Jeanne Shadwell, Evelyn Ruffin, Glennie Jean Miller, Bernice Peters, Betsy Brock, Mavolyn Brown and Wanda Jean Cevarich. *Front row:* Jacqueline Williams and Bettie Terrell. *Courtesy of Bettie Terrell Dorsey Hobson. Photograph by Whitaker Studio.*

You'd wink and say aloha to everyone you knew
Little hula hands we love you

The year 1958's *Melody of the Bells* depicted different types of bells: "Wedding Bells," "Trolley Bells," "Fire Bells," "Milk Maid Bells," "Sleigh Bells," "Winter Bells," "Town Crier Bells," "Bell of the Good Humor Man," "Class Bells" and "Ship Bells." The program started with "The Bells," a poem by Edgar Allan Poe.

Since the performers lived in Virginia, it made sense to highlight the Old Dominion, which is exactly what occurred in 1959's *A Book Revue of Virginia*, featuring "Garden Week in Virginia," "Cardinals," "Dainty Daffodils," "Violets," "Azaleas," "Smithfield, Virginia" (with "Peanuts" and "Virginia Ham") and many colleges and universities in the state: "Spirit of VMI," "Tech Triumphs," "Washington and Lee Fancy Dress Ball" ("Washington and Lee Swing"), "University of Richmond," "William & Mary," "Hampden Sydney" and "Randolph Macon." The city of Richmond wasn't left out. The "Spirit of Richmond" included dances called "Mosque Theatre," "Dogwood Dell," "Southern Biscuit Company" ("Lorna Doone Cookies" and "Scotch Short Bread") and "Tobacco Row."

The theme could be about greeting cards, like 1960's *Greetings and Best Wishes*. Of course, there were "Christmas Cards" and "New Years Cards" (with separate acts called "Snow Balls," "Mistletoe," "Christmas Trees," "Candy Canes" and "Happy New Year"), "Easter Cards" (with "Easter Baskets," "Easter Bonnets" and "Easter Lilies"), "Valentine Cards" ("Queen of Hearts," played by Joan Douglas Pemberton; "Who Stole My Heart Away?"; "Will My Arrow Find Your Heart?"; "Will You Be My Sweetheart?"; "Won't You Bee My Valentine?" and "Who Is Fencing Your Heart?") and "Saint Patrick's Day Cards" ("Too-Ra-Loo-Ra-Loo-Ral" and "The Luck of the Irish"). "April Fools Cards" appeared, with the words in the program foolishly printed upside down.

In 1963 audience members witnessed *Collectors' Items*, which included many of the typical collectibles, such as "Rare Coins" (and a chance to do "Pennies from Heaven," "Silver Coins" and "Gold Coins") "Stamps," "Sea Shells" and "Dolls & Toys" (including "Barbie Dolls," "Kewpie Dolls," "Little Women Dolls" and "Antique Jewelry"). "Salt & Pepper Shakers" rendered a skit, as did "Figurines," "Fans" and "Match Book Covers" (which spun off "Waldorf Astoria," "Play Boy Club," "Bunnies" and "Play Boys").

The Frylics could be about things that make you happy, like 1968's *Happiness Is*, in which happiness was depicted through the letters of the alphabet. Some letters got more than a single dance, and some dances introduced additional sub dances. For A, you had "All-American Girls," and B introduced "Birthday Party" (which spun off "Ice Cream" and "Cake"). The "Circus" and "Clowns" appeared for C, and D offered "Degas," "Dance Prints" and "Disneyland." From there, you had "Easter," "Fiesta" ("Fiesta Girls," "Tequila"), "Garden" (with "Farmers," "Scarecrows," "Carrots," "Lettuce," "Tomatoes"), "Hoboes," "Independence," "Jazzy," "Kitchen," "Les Sylphides," "Magic," "Nursery Rhymes," "Oil Painting," "Parade," "Quartette," "Retirement," "Sailing," "Travelogue," "Umbrella," "Valentine," "Winter," "Xylophone" and "Young at Heart" (sung by Jane Ellen Tyler). "Zest" finished up the alphabet.

The variety seems endless: several routines concerned transportation, such as 1950's "Mule Train," "Bicycle Built for Two," "The Trolley Song," "Chattanooga Choo-Choo," "Airplane" and "In My Merry Oldsmobile," with dancers pedaling across the stage on tandem bicycles. This number also featured a father in a Frylics—in this case, William (Bill) Bickerstaff riding a high-wheel penny-farthing, one of those old-fashioned bicycles with the huge oversized front wheel. There was an act called "Cherubs and a Guilty Conscious," which revealed twelve girls as cherubs and Linda Salsbury as the "Little Guilty Conscious," who unsuccessfully tried to entice the cherubs into wickedness.

And on it goes. They even had dances for selecting the name for a newborn baby. Who would have thought you could put thirty-two children in creative costumes performing "Sweet Sue"? Then, sixteen more performed "Mary," and before it was over, the dancers amused the assemblage with separate dances for "Dinah," "Cecilia," "Louisa" and "Rosalie."

If someone tells you he or she danced for Miss Fry, don't be surprised to hear that person (with a laugh) performed as a carrot, a stamp or a Degas print.

The theme could be magazines, like 1965's *Out of the Magazine Rack*. Certainly there's enough material for dozens of dances. Each magazine spun off separate numbers, so the "Sports Illustrated" dance introduced "Baseball" and "Boating." "Art Magazine" introduced "Lavender," and "The New Yorker" brought in a delightful array, including "Give My Regards to Broadway" and "Play Boys." "Hunting Magazine" depicted "Hunters" (with the fox played by Linda Marker), while "Virginia Wildlife Magazine" featured "DO-RE-MI" and "Does—Female Deer" (with Joanna Forrest Parker, Paula Neal and Laura Crowder). A photograph of Laura Crowder as a "Doe-a Deer" (in a brown sleeveless leotard with a huge spot on the front and a hat with ears tied under her chin) was used years later for the invitation for her surprise fiftieth birthday party. Other Wildlife numbers included "Rays of Golden Sun," "Chipmunks," "Bunnies," "Golden Pheasants," "Cardinals," "Frogs" and even something called "Hobo Life"— which presented ten kids as hoboes.

Edith Lindeman Reviews

Edith Lindeman of the *Times-Dispatch* wrote some fabulous reviews about the recitals, which she (or a *Times-Dispatch* editor) often incorrectly referred to as Frylicks rather than Frylics. The reviews included many of the performers' names with highlights of some of the dances, and she was always delighted the shows did not drag on endlessly. Ms. Lindeman started writing reviews of film and theatre for the *Times-Dispatch* in 1933 and retired in 1964. You get the feeling she must have had to sit through some awfully long children's shows. She could not have been more pleased that the Frylics were not only exceptionally creative but also crisp and efficient. The 1939 show, according to Ms. Lindeman, included

*an exquisite Ballet of the Flowers with some excellent toe work...
One number had a dozen girls posturing before mirrors, while their
"reflections" proved to be fellow dancers...Colorful as ever, sped
through with a facile promptness that marks Miss Fry's dance revues
and tricked out with several effective backdrops, the show ticked off a
score of numbers...Once again Miss Fry has added to her laurels and
to the enjoyment of her Richmond audiences.*[82]

The 1940 show, Ms. Lindeman raved, featured "the same swift, clear-cut
performance always associated with this group."[83] An unidentified writer
(but probably Ms. Lindeman) opined in 1934 that the show

*add[ed] new laurels to Miss Fry's reputation as a danseuse and
instructor...The show moved with speed and brilliance. The late curtains
and long waits often noticed in amateur performances were happily absent,
and the 3-year-olds as well as the graduate pupils went into their dances
quickly, did their steps and took their bows with the aplomb one expects from
those with long stage experience...The young steppers...deserve laudatory
adjectives...but even to render praise where praise is due is dangerous when
there are 300 or more children involved. What if one praised the light toe
work and shimmering costumes of the snowflakes and forgot to say kind
words about the even more exquisite Degas ballet?... "Doing the Uptown
Lowdown" was a hot Harlem number but there were some other hot-cha
dances that went over just as big...Miss Fry's two dances—"Steppin'
the Steps" and "The Rainbow"—merited all the applause they received
and that was enough to stop the show twice...Frylics was a good show
presented for a worthy cause to an enthusiastic audience, and citing one more
reason for praise, we close: Frylics was kept in a two-hour limit which is
reason enough to laud it to the skies.*[84]

A reviewer named Helen de Motte, identified in her newspaper byline
as "H de M," claimed the 1934 show was a "well-planned, swift moving,
compact production upon which Miss Fry is to be especially congratulated...
an extremely artistic production as well, the costumes being exquisite both
in color and design."[85]

VI

MOMENTS TO REMEMBER

"MR. FRY"

The papers announced the engagement on August 3, 1941. At 8:00 p.m. on September 6, 1941, Reverend Beverley Munford Boyd married Frances Elinor Fry and Stuart Wesley Phillips at Grace and Holy Trinity Church, the church where Elinor Fry had been baptized on June 14, 1916.

Elinor and Stuart had known each other since childhood. She was given in marriage by her mother. Mrs. William Amonette Terrell, Miss Fry's sister, was matron of honor, and the other bridesmaids were Mrs. Bernard Winn McCary and Miss Edith Phillips. Miss Bettie Jane Terrell was the junior bridesmaid. A reception followed at the Commonwealth Club, and then Mr. and Mrs. Phillips set off on a motor trip to Maine. When they returned in late September (in time for Miss Fry/Mrs. Phillips to start dance lessons), they moved into the guest cottage at Ballyshannon, a mansion overlooking the James River, owned by friends. Stuart Phillips (born September 28, 1898) was a banker with State Planners Bank. It was the only marriage for each of them.

In February 1942, the *Times-Dispatch* carried a story of brides from prior years. The article contained a photograph of Miss Fry, accompanied with the words: "Moonlight and roses, and to you a gentle sigh; this is Mrs. Stuart Phillips, the former Elinor Fry."[86] Her pupils still called her Miss Fry, even after the wedding. In fact, they often referred to her husband as Mr. Fry. According to former pupils, he was an elegant, poised and

The Elinor Fry School of The Dance
1920 THROUGH 1970

Proudly Presents This

Certificate of Merit

To

Stuarl Wesley Phillips . Head Master.

At the Closing of the School this First Day of May,
Nineteen Hundred and Seventy-One

Elinor Fry.

complete gentleman, who often stopped in to say hello, bring a box of cookies or candy for the girls to enjoy after a show or deliver dinner to his wife. Nancy Ogg Tripp said he was always there on the sidelines. He dressed very well, usually with a tie and a vest, and was very kind to everyone. Roger Riggle Jr. characterized him as having a "Churchill-type look." Miss Fry found a place in several numbers over the years for her husband. In the 1963 Frylics, he sang "Honeybun" in a *South Pacific* routine, and in 1965 he sang "Vaudeville."

In April 1970, Miss Fry talked about her upcoming retirement. One of the reasons given was her husband's health; at the time, he was recovering from a heart attack.[87] Miss Fry probably awarded many handwritten certificates in her five decades of teaching, but her husband may have received the very last one, a Certificate of Merit to "Headmaster" Stuart Wesley Phillips: "At the closing of the School this first day of May, Nineteen hundred and seventy-one." Stuart W. Phillips, "Mr. Fry," died on April 16, 1981, and was buried at Hollywood Cemetery.

MISS FRY RETIRES

In April 1970, the *News Leader* did a story about Miss Fry, when she was sixty-seven. Miss Fry, the article noted, "retains the dancer's quality of youthfulness. Her eyes are twinkling, clear, her fair complexion flawless, her laugh quick. To all appearances, her energy and patience are limitless."[88]

In the Frylics of 1970, Miss Fry performed a solo "Butterfly" and danced "Soaring" with several of her longtime assistants. She knew at the time that the 1970 recital, *Moments to Remember*, would be the last one, so it's no surprise that it relied on her favorite routines from over the years, including, of course, "Moonlight and Roses."

St. Catherine's recognized Miss Fry in April 1970 with the Distinguished Alumna Award for "giving of her talents in the true spirit of the school motto: 'What we keep we lose, only what we give remains our own.'" The school originally opened in 1890 as the Virginia Randolph Ellett School. It changed its name to St. Catherine's in the year Miss Fry graduated: 1920. I met with Sarah Martin Herguner, the school's archivist, to see what Miss Fry–related documents the school might have. Lucky for me, Sarah, a St. Catherine's graduate (class of '77), wanted to uncover material as much as I wanted her to uncover it. She indefatigably rifled through her trove of folders to come up with several great finds, including photographs and a handwritten letter from Miss Fry:

When I received the notice from St. Catherine's that this would be the fiftieth anniversary of my graduation—I suddenly realized that this would also be my fiftieth year of teaching dancing—I knew I had been teaching for a long time—for dancing has happily absorbed the greater part of my life—but I did not realize how long! I started studying when I was three or four years old from Miss Ella Binford—but had to stop when my father passed away. Later I took from Miss Idear Steele Traylor and from Miss Anne Boyer. It was a wonderful experience and I enjoyed being in many of the Tray-Boy recitals. I was proud to have been—along with Berkeley Davis—the first to graduate from the Tray-Boy School of Dance. It was a great loss to Richmond when Miss Traylor died several years ago. Miss Boyer—I'm happy to say is still teaching in Danville, Virginia—and carrying on her splendid work. With the help of my wonderful mother I started my studio in 1920—the same year I graduated from St. Catherine's. I was a member of the Little Theatre League and I will never forget the thrill of having the leading role in one of Mr. James Branch Cabell's plays—"The

Jewel Merchants" and also in Captain Applejack, etc...Another important moment to remember was the Beaux Art competitions which were held in all branches of the arts—dancing, music, painting, singing, etc. I was very proud of my pupils—for my school won both of the bronze medals—one for dancers 8 to 14 and the other for dancers over 16. We also won 21 blue ribbons...In 1933 I put on our first "Frylics." It was given for the benefit of the Virginia Association of Workers for the Blind. I had been teaching volunteer classes for the blind and 8 of the girls danced in the recital and most of the audience didn't even realize they were blind. Can you imagine the thrill it was for me to have had Miss Helen Keller and teacher Miss Sullivan to appear in my first recital? In 1941 Stuart W. Phillips and I were married—he was so wonderful and understanding that I continued teaching. But we had no recitals during World War II—because I was

St. Catherine's fiftieth reunion—class of 1920. *Courtesy of St. Catherine's School and J. Etheridge Ward.*

so busy as a volunteer Red Cross worker—we also put on shows with the Bond-a-liers to help sell war bonds. After the war the Richmond Chapter of the American Legion asked me to give the recital for their benefit to raise money to help carry on their splendid work at McGuire's Hospital. I donate all of my time, in fact they couldn't pay me for the great amount of time I spend on the Frylics—but I feel that we are helping those who have given so much for us. I am so very grateful that I had the opportunity of being one of "Miss Jennies' Girls" and of being able to attend St. Catherine's wonderful school. I am also most grateful to have had many, many wonderful students—their fine families—and such a fine staff of associates, teachers and accompanists—for without them I would not have so many "Moments to Remember."[89]

In 1975, her dance studio came to a final end when she donated her remaining dance items to St. Catherine's. The school thanked her for

the most intriguing of items which you so kindly donated to the theatre department...The ribbons and net and trimmings all sound very useful and ought to add color and interest to productions...for years to come. I am intrigued too by the array of hats! Irish, pilgrim, beadle and plastic boy hats! It is a wonderfully thoughtful thing for you to do...and I write to say a very warm thank you.[90]

The Elinor Fry Phillips '20 Fund was established in 1984 with money bequeathed to the school in Miss Fry's will. To this day, the fund is still supporting the dance program at St. Catherine's and is used specifically to bring in guest artists (dance teachers/choreographers) from outside the school community and/or to help provide off-campus dance education opportunities for its students.

Bill Hazelgrove shared with me a photo of Miss Fry "teaching" a can-can in the late 1960s to about twenty Richmond business and civic leaders. The mirthful event was called the *Swine Lake Ballet*, a play on Swan Lake. You can almost hear the laughter in the photo, everyone hamming it up for charity and having a wonderful time. Miss Fry, the only woman in the photo, is doing a split that no one over the age of twenty should ever try. Miss Fry also performed in a "Vaudeville Is Back" show at the Jefferson Hotel in September 1970.

Lina Lee Bacigalupo Butler said that once Miss Fry retired, the magic was gone. Many pupils continued to see her around town, at various events, doing

"Teaching" some old guys, circa 1970—laughing, dancing and raising money for charity. *Courtesy of Bill Hazelgrove.*

her good deeds. Suffering at the end with Alzheimer's, she died at age eighty in her home on January 8, 1984, the same day as her niece Bettie Terrell Dorsey Hobson's birthday. Mrs. Hobson remarked about how honored and privileged she felt to be introduced as Elinor Fry's niece: "To have her as a role model was overwhelming at times. All of us cherish our own special memories of her." Mrs. Hobson's daughter, Terry Dorsey Dalton, stated that "although 'Aunt El' did not have any biological children, she touched the lives of countless children and positively influenced each one. She was creative, generous, caring—truly an amazing woman."

Upon hearing the news, Margaret Woodburn, a former pupil and assistant, wrote that any child touched by Miss Fry was richer for life.[91]

Grayson Jones added, "From the time she started teaching, the little ones, after doing their curtsies at the end of the class, could hardly wait to swamp her with hugs. Miss Fry became like a mother hen engulfing her biddies as she spread her arms around them with love. The pupils' love for her was and still is a most rewarding tribute to the great lady."[92]

The following letter was in Miss Fry's scrapbook. Unfortunately, I wasn't able to determine who wrote it:

Learning to Dance

The joy of learning to dance came at an early age, when I was five years old. I had always wanted to learn to dance, especially ballet. I kept asking my mother, or to be more precise, bugging her to let me take up dancing. Then came the happy day after mother finally consented. Her servant, Lilly, walked me up to Miss Fry's dance studio. I was so happy that I just could not wait. Lilly helped me with dressing and putting on my new pink leotard and black shiny tap shoes. She also brought me a new ballet bag with my name on it. Inside the bag was my new pair of ballet slippers. When we got to the studio there were lots of other excited girls and boys. Miss Fry and her helpers got us together and set around the floor. She asked each of us to tell our names. After we told our names we all got up and stood in a line until Miss Fry's helpers got out a mat. This was called an exercise session. We learned how to get down on our knees, tuck our heads down and roll over. The straight line was a bit crooked, being the first time most of us went off the mat. The next thing we were instructed to do was lie down on the mats on our stomachs. Miss Fry's helpers stood behind us. Can you believe they wanted us to put our hands back and pull both feet up behind us? Yes, we tried to touch our heads to our toes. Some of us could accomplish this remarkable feat while others just rolled over in laughter. By the time my class was over I began to have little tears in my eyes. I was having too much fun to stop and go home. I went back to the changing room, put on my slacks and blouse. My maid walked me home. When I got home mother was excited. The first thing she asked was, "How was your first day at dancing school?" I was just so happy, jumping up and down, I could not answer her at first. But after I calmed down somewhat I finally did. Unknown to me I had walked home with my tap shoes on. I told mother that I did not want to take them off. There was quite a fuss because I refused to take them off until the following Saturday. I cried and pouted. Mother talked to me for a long time. At last I decided to take my shoes off and put them into my ballet bag. Such a happy ending to such a wonderful day.[93]

Robert Watkins, the artistic director for the Concert Ballet of Virginia wrote:

Elinor, With Dearest Love…

In the past few weeks I have been reading [Elinor Fry's] scrapbooks, letters of thanks and commendations and programs and now I realize that I am merely one among hundreds whose spirits have been raised by her apparently endless ability to be thoughtful, kind, generous and there at the right moment.

The scrapbooks reveal performing credits so voluminous and varied that it is difficult to say when the performing began…it must have been in the early twenties, just about the time she opened her dancing school with six pupils…by 1933 the Frylics was an established tradition and an advertisement promised "a gorgeous dancing singing spectacle" in the Mosque each spring told the truth for many, many years.

At the beginning each student's photograph appeared in miniature on the program with Miss Fry in the center. As the enrollment grew the pictures diminished in size, but were there until her studio grew beyond the hope of including everyone's photograph in the entire program book. But they were always in her thoughts and her awareness of individual personal and professional needs never failed.

She managed to find time to remain in spotlights other than that of teacher and the scrapbooks reveal her acting in a little theatre production, piloting an airplane, appearing in a grand historical pageant, dancing on a full scale airplane at a Governor's Ball, participating in war bond drives in World War II and performing for service men and in military hospitals.

But for me her most spectacular appearance was when, at the famous Beaux Arts Ball of 1932 in the Jefferson, she descended from the ceiling of the grand foyer in a glass sphere and emerged in diaphanous draperies to dance for the richly caparisoned guests.

What a life…she had it all here in Richmond! Of course she was blessed to live in an era when creative accomplishments by a native were a source of wonder in the community and she created and performed to the hilt. Such a career that went almost into seven decades was a wondrous gift and her stewardship of this gift was faultless.

I last saw her when she came to a Sunday matinee of our "Swan Lake" last November…she took my hand and kissed it and that kiss will never go away. Long ago a Richmond poet, Duval Porter, celebrated her beauty and talent in a sonnet with lines that might well be our salute to her:
Sweet maiden, Thou of soulful eyes
And happy heart, may sunny skies
Look down on Thee where e'er Thou art…[94]

Patsy Bickerstaff wrote the following poem; it was published in 1993 in the *Ariel XII*, a publication of Triton College.

La Sylphide
(In memory of Elinor Fry Phillips)

Along the barre,
blooming ruffled pink blossom buds,
her lambswool voice,
her white-bird hands
moved tiptoe soft,
nurturing to grace
freckled fingers,
scraped tomboy knees,
lifted us
just above the floor, where she lived.
Godmother, spirit, butterfly,
healer of small bones.
adolescent hearts,
by sequin-satin magic,
music,
fantasy.
Bend in, lean out, plié, reach up.
This hour, no words existed
for ugly, stupid, stuckup,
clumsy, skinny, fat,
only sounds like honey in the room.
All were stars,
the smallest child a giant.
She touched us;
like Christmas dolls
we warmed to life,
danced:
glissade, arabesque,
around the island,
sandari,
mazurka,
tinikling,
tiny taps applauding themselves.

Running to her arms,
we must have known
only one love
could tether such a sky-bound soul to earth;
that anchor loosed,
we stood embracing images of light,
watching her fly away
like gossamer,
like wilis on wind.[95]

EPILOGUE

Many of Miss Fry's former students are still out there on stage, dancing and entertaining. Patsy Bickerstaff participates in international folk dance, Linda Salsbury Weinstein teaches ballroom dance, Patsy Garrett does 1940s routines in her California senior center, Jacqueline Goldberg Jones directs and performs as an actress, Roger Riggle Jr. directs and choreographs musical operas and Romy Nordlinger performs on television, film and stage. I'm sure there are many more. Miss Fry would be proud beyond measure of all her pupils. She would be thrilled to know they are still laughing and having fun, while carrying on her tradition of giving back and doing good.

An April 1970 article claimed her life and dancing career were as bright as the brilliant extravaganza display of her dance revues. "It really makes me very sad to even think about it, but—" Miss Fry quietly said as her voice trailed off—"I will never forget the thrill..."[96]

Helen Coleman spoke for all of Miss Fry's friends, family and former pupils when she said, "I still marvel at her endless patience and boundless love...Indeed, we are fortunate to have known this talented, generous lady, our Miss Fry."[97]

This note to her students captures the guidance she instilled:

> *Your life lies before you like a field of new fallen snow—so—be careful what you do and where you go—for every foot step will surely show! Wishing you good health, much happiness and a special good bye—from your devoted friend—Elinor Fry.*[98]

TIMELINE

1898   May 11: Peter Meriwether Fry Jr. is born.

September 28: Stuart Wesley Phillips is born.

1899   September 17: Virginia Fry, Miss Fry's sister, is born.

1903   July 23: Elinor Fry is born.

1906   August 25: Miss Fry performs as "Little Miss Muffet" in a "Mother Goose" costume party in Natural Bridge, Virginia.

1909   April 23: Miss Fry and other pupils of Miss Ella Binford (and Lillian Binford) dance at the Jefferson Hotel.

1910   April 2: Miss Fry dances the "Kindergarten Polka" in the "Mother Goose" carnival at the Jefferson Hotel.

April 14: Miss Fry dances at the Fancy Dress Ball at Belvidere Hall.

July 31: From Natural Bridge, Virginia: "A charming event of the week was the birthday party of little Miss Elinor Fry."

1911   January 11: Miss Fry's father, Peter Meriwether Fry, dies.

April 19: Miss Ella Binford's pupils, including Elinor Fry and Virginia Fry, perform at the Fancy Dress Ball at Belvidere Hall.

1914   December 13: Advertisement in a newspaper for a lost dog, Buster—a small, brown and white pet bull terrier (call Elinor Fry, Madison 3950-L).

1915 April 24: Miss Fry is among Miss Binford's dancers performing at the Blues' Bazaar.

1916 February 16: Miss Fry, a pupil of Miss Binford, does a "Skirt Dance" at the Jefferson Hotel.

April 28: Miss Fry performs "The Hesitation" toe dance at the Jefferson Hotel; Misses Elinor Fry and Gwendolyn Seldon do "Shadow Dance" in *Vanity Fair* at the Jefferson Hotel.

June 1–3: Miss Fry, a pupil of Miss Binford, performs a gypsy dance and a Spanish dance at an Indoor Garden Party at the Masonic Temple.

November 24: Miss Fry and her sister Virginia Fry participate in a charity tea for the United Daughters of the Confederacy.

1917 February 4: The *Times-Dispatch* publishes several drawings done by children, including one of a child skating, done by Elinor Fry.

February 14: Miss Fry dances at the Jefferson Hotel Valentine's Day Party.

April 10: Miss Fry, a student of Miss Binford, performs a solo dance at "Holiday Ball" at the Jefferson Hotel.

1919 May 14: Miss Fry performs a solo dance in "Snowball Minstrels" in the new schoolhouse at Ginter Park.

May 23–24: Miss Binford brings a cast of 150 to dance in "Toyland" to benefit Sheltering Arms Hospital.

1921 February 20: Miss Fry performs in James Branch Cabell's *The Rivet in Grandfather's Neck*, hosted by Little Theatre League.

June 21: Miss Fry plays the leading woman in James Branch Cabell's *The Jewel Merchant*.

November 15: Winners are named for the statewide voting for Queen of the Virginia Historical Pageant. Miss Fry didn't win queen but won "Maid of Honor" for the third congressional district.

November 29–30: Miss Fry performs in several roles in *The Merry Wheel of 1921*.

1922 May 22–28: Miss Fry plays the Spirit of the Virgin Land in the Virginia Historical Pageant.

June 20: Miss Fry serves as assistant maid of honor for Thirty-second Confederate Reunion.

October 1: Miss Fry is presented to society as a debutante.

October 30: Miss Fry attends (with Clarence Boykin) the *Tangerine* at the Academy of Music.

November 1: Miss Fry attends a luncheon in honor of Miss Dorothy Meek, debutante, at the Rose Bowl Inn.

November 3: Miss Fry is honored at tea by her sister, Mrs. William Amonette Terrell (formerly Miss Virginia Fry).

November 7: Miss Fry is named to serve on the entertainment committee for UDC, Lee Chapter, Christmas week.

November 15: Miss Fry attends (but does not perform in) Gilbert & Sullivan's *Pinafore* at the Academy of Music.

November 19: Tray Boy's advanced pupils give demonstrations all week; the first dance (with Miss Fry) is "Ocean at Sunrise."

November 25: Miss Fry is a guest of honor (along with Miss Cyane Bemiss) at a luncheon.

November 30: Miss Fry and others travel to Charlottesville for a football game and dance.

December 11: Miss Fry is listed as a debutante of the season at the opening of the German Club at the Jefferson Hotel.

December 22: Miss Fry is presented to formal Richmond society at a brilliant function at the Jefferson Hotel.

1923　April 12–14: Miss Fry performs several specialty dances in the Frolics of '23 at the Strand.

May 16: Miss Fry performs as a "Blue Bird" in the James River Garden Club's Flower Show.

Frolics of 1923, sponsored by the American Legion at the Strand, are led by local stars of recognized talent such as the delightful Elinor Fry.

December 22: Miss Fry gives a tea at her studio at 2600 Monument Avenue in honor of Miss Margaret Burwell.

1924　February 12: Miss Fry and her mother return from Lexington, where Miss Fry attended mid-winter dances and the Fancy Dress Ball at the Virginia Military Institute.

March 5: Miss Fry assists at a tea in honor of Miss Virginia Archer Page.

July 24: Miss Fry returns home after a week in Frederick's Hall, where she was the guest of Miss Marjorie Terrell.

November 26: Miss Fry dances at Westhampton College.

December 6: Miss Fry gives a tea in honor of Miss Hildreth Scott.

December 11: Miss Fry's pupils—called "Miss Fry's Dancing Dollies"—perform in the *Black Cat Minstrels* at the Academy of Music.

December 19: Miss Fry performs in the Little Theatre League's *Dover Road*.

1925   February 9: Two of Miss Fry's pupils, Miss Floyd Ward and Marvin Powell, dance at the Richmond Hotel's Winter Garden.

March 9: Miss Fry's pupils dance at the Richmond Hotel's Winter Garden for UDC, Lee Chapter.

April 2–4: The Little Theatre League presents Frolics of '25 at the Strand. Miss Fry's students do a "Russian Dance." This annual show is sponsored by the American Legion.

April 19: Miss Fry's pupils dance in the College Club of Richmond's "The Mollusc [*sic*]."

April 27: Miss Fry's pupils dance in a fashion show at the Richmond Hotel's Winter Garden to benefit the Sheltering Arms Free Hospital.

May 12: Miss Marjorie Hemingway, a pupil of Miss Fry, dances in *A Southern Cinderella* at Patrick Henry School.

June 22–24: The Richmond Hotel's Winter Garden hosts dance shows with two of Miss Fry's advanced students, Marjorie Hemingway and Emily Thompson.

October 13: Miss Fry is one of the servers for the Golden Rule dinner at the Richmond Hotel's Winter Garden.

November 12: Miss Fry's dancers and Miss Binford's dancers perform for the Community Fund at the Academy of Music.

December 5: Miss Fry's pupils dance in the Blue Bazaar Circus.

December 17: Miss Fry's pupils dance at American Legion Post #1.

December 20: Miss Fry dances in *The Romancers* at the Little Theatre League.

1926 January 9: Miss Fry gives tea at her Monument Avenue studio in honor of Misses Mary Bell Miller and Cordon Fry.

March 12: Miss Fry's pupils dance for the Richmond Automobile Club.

April 14: Several of Miss Fry's pupils dance in the Frolics of '26 at John Marshall High School, sponsored by the American Legion.

April 26: Miss Fry's student Miss Virginia Garrett performs a solo dance at the Soldiers' Home.

June 4: Miss Fry's pupils dance at Brook Hill, under the auspices of Grace and Trinity Church and the Juniors of Emmanuel Church.

June 30: Miss Fry is the guest of Mrs. Barton Grundy in Bar Harbor, Maine.

September 30: Miss Fry's pupils dance at an event for officers and men of the Richmond Naval Reserves.

October 21: Miss Fry's pupils dance at the Grandchildren's Chapter of the UDC at the Soldiers' Home.

October 24: Miss Fry, recovering from an operation for appendicitis, leaves her dancing classes under the supervision of the older pupils.

December 29: Virginia Garrett dances at the National Theatre in a troupe with more than eighteen of Miss Fry's pupils in *A Mid-Winter Fantasy*.

1927 February 1: Miss Fry's pupils dance at the Richmond Hotel's Winter Garden for Lions Club Ladies' Night.

February 18: Miss Fry's pupils dance at a tea during National Drama Week at the Community Theatre.

February 20: Miss Fry's pupils—Emily Thompson, Mary Griffith, Thelma Pate, Mary Todd and Anita Wyland—perform at Ladies' Night "Grotto" at the Elks Home.

March 4: Miss Annabel Spolkin, Miss Fry's pupil, dances for event at YW and YMHA [*sic*].

April 4: Miss Fry's pupils dance for the Music Conference.

April 4–9: Miss Fry's pupils dance *In Old Vienna*.

April 10: Four of Miss Fry's pupils dance for a benefit for Sheltering Arms Hospital.

April 20: Miss Fry's pupils dance at Cathedral's Boys' School for Sacred Hearts Alumna Association.

April 29–30: Miss Fry pupils dance in *Captain Applejack* at the Strand, hosted by the Little Theatre League.

May 2: Miss Fry's pupils dance for UDC, Stonewall Jackson Chapter, at the Richmond Hotel's Winter Garden.

May 11: Miss Fry's pupils dance for Dove Rebecca Lodge.

May 21: Miss Fry's pupils dance at a banquet at the Jefferson Hotel.

May 26: Miss Fry's pupils dance in the late afternoon at Paxton, the Cary Street home of Mrs. John Skelton, and also that evening some pupils dance at a banquet at the Jefferson Hotel for the American Pulp and Paper Mills Superintendents' Association.

May 27: Miss Fry's pupils dance at the Children's Theatre *Cinderella* at the William Fox School.

June 1: Miss Fry's pupils dance at Sauer's Japanese Garden during a convention of the Flavoring Extract Manufacturers' Association.

June 8: The *Times-Dispatch* features Miss Fry in an article about Richmond women working outside their homes.

June 9: Miss Fry's pupils dance at the "Shrine Century Ball" at Grays' Armory.

June 17: Miss Fry's pupils dance at Pollard Park for the Richmond Junior Chapter, UDC.

August 7: The *Times-Dispatch* prints sketch (by Von Jost) of Miss Fry.

August 11: Miss Mary Todd, pupil of Miss Fry, teaches a burlesque number for *The Pink Cat*.

October 20: Miss Fry's pupils dance at a Community Fund event.

October 25: Miss Fry's pupils dance at the Jefferson Hotel for a convention of the Associated Traffic Clubs of America.

November 2: Miss Fry's pupils dance at Highland Springs Junior High School for the Daughters of Liberty.

November 4: Miss Fry's pupils dance at the Petersburg Lions Club "Ladies' Night."

December 29–31: Miss Fry and twenty-six of her pupils perform in *Jazzmania* at the Mosque.

1928   January 31: Miss Fry and a group of her pupils dance *In the Storm* at the Washington and Lee University's Twenty-second Annual Fancy Dress Ball.

February 20: Miss Fry and her advanced pupils dance for the George Washington Ball at the armory, including "A Dutch Dance" and a feature with fifty young couples dressed in colonial costumes.

March 16: Miss Fry's pupils dance at the Richmond Chapter, UDC pageant at John Marshall High School.

March 17: Miss Fry's pupils dance at the Mosque in *How Knowledge Drives Away Fears*, hosted by the Richmond Safety Council.

May 12: Miss Fry hosts closing exercises for her pupils at the Richmond Hotel's Winter Garden.

May 18–19: Miss Fry's pupils dance in Adventure Days; this ends with "Memories of the Centuries" at Swan Island in Shield's Lake.

May 26: Miss Fry's pupils dance at Mosby Auditorium for the Grey Lantern Players' *The Rescue of Princess Winsome.*

June 1: Miss Fry's "scarf and nature pupils" dance for the Teachers Auxiliary of Second Baptist Church.

October 5: Miss Fry's pupils dance at the Governor's Ball at Grays' Armory under the auspices of the Virginia League of Women Voters.

October 7: Miss Fry's dancers do a minuet at Monticello; photographs of this appear in the April 1929 issue of *National Geographic.*

October 21: Miss Fry's former pupils—Miss Thompson, Miss Wyland and Hertha Bryant—appear at the National in *Along Broadway* all this week.

November 10: Miss Fry's pupils dance in *Sleeping Beauty*, hosted by the Children's Theatre.

December 15: Miss Fry's pupils dance at the intermission for a ball for Miss Elizabeth Green at the Country Club of Virginia.

December 22: Miss Fry gives a Christmas party for her pupils at the Richmond Hotel's Winter Garden.

December 31: Miss Fry's pupils dance at the Byrd Theatre.

1929   February 12: An advertisement to "Hear and See Fox Movietone News including Elinor Fry's Little Dancing Girls" appears.

February 18: Miss Fry is listed as one of fifteen contestants for the Popular Lady contest, as part of the Shrine Circus at the Mosque.

February 20: Miss Fry and her pupils dance *In a Little Garden* at the Little Theatre League.

February 21: Miss Fry's pupils dance at the Commonwealth Club for the American Institute of Bankers.

February 22: Miss Fry and two of her dancers perform "Dance Orientale" and "Tale of the Dancing Girl" in Washington and Lee University's Twenty-fourth Annual Fancy Dress Ball.

February 22: Miss Fry's pupils dance at the Colonial Ball at the armory.

February 28: Miss Fry and her pupils dance in a Jonas Style Revue at the Byrd Theatre.

March 21: Miss Fry performs at the Sphinx Club at the Seventh Street Christian Church Annex.

April 6: Miss Fry's pupils dance in *The Giant's Gumdrop* at the Women's Theatre.

April 9–10: Miss Fry's pupils dance in a minstrel show for St. Benedict's Mothers' Club.

April 11: Miss Fry's pupils dance as dolls and wooden soldiers at a "Mother Goose Party" to benefit the Holy Comforter Church.

April 12: Shirley Cadmus, one of Miss Fry's pupils, performs at a "Pink Tea" given by the Imp Club of the John Marshall High School.

April 16: Miss Fry dances in *The Marriage of Pocahontas and John Rolfe* at Swan Island in Byrd Park to close the Adventure Day's program.

April 16: The tenth-anniversary celebration of the American Legion in Virginia is held at the Richmond Hotel's Winter Garden.

April 19: Miss Fry's pupils dance at WRVA Corn Cob Pipe Club at North Side School.

April 24: Miss Fry's pupils perform at the Richmond Hotel's Winter Garden for two hundred employees of the Cohen Company—for "a dance and "whoopee."

April 27: Miss Fry hosts a tea at the Country Club of Virginia in honor of Miss Irma Duncan and the Isodora Duncan Dancers.

June 21: Miss Fry's pupils dance for the Virginia Bankers Association at Chamberlin-Vanderbilt Hotel, Old Point Comfort.

June 27: Miss Fry's pupils dance on the USS *Richmond* in Hampton Roads, Virginia.

June 29: Miss Fry's pupils dance at the North Side Post of the American Legion Auxiliary.

October 25: A *Times-Dispatch* article about pilots carries a photograph of Elinor Fry and a picture of her brother, Meriwether.

November 1: Miss Fry performs "Aeroplane Dance" for the Second Annual Governor's Ball at John Marshall Hotel.

November 21: Miss Fry's pupils dance at UDC, Janet Randolph Chapter.

1930   January 16: Miss Fry's pupils dance for a state chamber of commerce meeting.

January 31: Miss Fry and some of her pupils dance at Washington and Lee University's Fancy Dress Ball.

February 21: Miss Fry's pupils dance at the J.E.B. Stuart School.

March 15: Miss Fry's pupils model clothes at Thalhimer's Fashion Show.

April 21: A story mentions that Miss Fry will soon have her pilot's license.

May 1: *Pageant at Swan Lake* features a dance of Indian maidens directed by Miss Fry.

May 27: Miss Fry's pupils model gowns from Greentrees at a fashion show at Byrd Theatre this week.

November 23: Miss Fry's pupils dance at the Hotel Richmond's Winter Garden.

1931   January 21: Miss Fry's pupils dance at the Confederate Ball at the John Marshall Hotel.

February 20: Miss Fry's pupils dance on the Roof Garden of the John Marshall Hotel for the American Institute of Bankers.

February 27: Miss Fry's pupils dance at a cabaret at the Mosque.

April 15: The Tournament of Arts Contest at Thomas Jefferson High School ends in a tie between an acrobatic group from Elinor Fry School and a military buck trio from Tray-Boy.

June 28: Miss Fry's brother, Peter M. Fry Jr. ("Meriwether"), dies in an airplane crash.

October 19: Miss Fry's pupils dance at the Governor's Ball.

1932   April 8: Miss Fry's pupils dance in a musical comedy to benefit the YWCA.

April 16: Miss Fry's dancers sweep the Tournament of Arts competition at Thomas Jefferson High School.

April 27: At the Beaux Arts Ball at the Jefferson Hotel, Miss Fry is lowered from the ceiling in a mammoth and modernistic tulip at the stroke of midnight.

November 12: Miss Fry's pupils dance in the Elks' Revue at the Mosque.

November 22: Miss Fry's pupils perform a minuet in colonial costumes at the Jefferson Hotel.

December 17: Miss Fry hosts a Christmas party at the John Marshall Hotel.

1933   May 20: Frylics of '33. This is the first Frylics recital.

August 8: The *Los Angeles Evening Herald and Express* reports that Miss Fry has become an ardent aviatrix, holding a pilot's license, and often goes up in her own plane in Richmond.

1934   April 18: Four of Miss Fry's pupils dance at the Race Ball at the Jefferson Hotel for the Deep Run Hunt Club.

May 4: Frylics of '34.

May 5: Fifty members of Miss Fry's Cotillion Club, who are dancing in the Frylics, dance in *Play Fiddle Play* at the Mosque.

May 31: Several of Miss Fry's pupils dance in gypsy costumes at Bellendean Fair, at the Chesterfield County home, Bellendean, of Mrs. Walter Scott.

August 1: The *Daily Sketch* publishes a story about Miss Fry and other American dance instructors in London.

1935   February 14: Miss Fry's pupils dance at the John Marshall Hotel for the Retail Coal Merchants Association.

February 18: Miss Fry's pupils dance at the Tantilla Garden for an A&P employees' party.

March 21: Miss Fry's pupils dance at the Mosque for the National Safety Council.

May 18: Frylics of '35.

May 21: Miss Fry's pupils present "Pipes of Pan" at Ballyshannon for the Association for Preservation of Virginia Antiquities.

May 21: Miss Fry's pupils dance at the John Marshall Hotel's Roof Garden for "Ladies' Night," sponsored by the East End Business Men's Association.

June 7: Miss Fry's pupils dance at the John Marshall Hotel for the American Pulp and Paper Mills Superintendents' Convention.

June 26: Miss Fry's pupils dance at the commencement of Marie Frick Costello's School of Music at the John Marshall Hotel's Roof Garden.

1936 January 2: William Amonette Terrell, Miss Fry's brother-in-law, passes away.

April 12: The *Times-Dispatch* carries a photograph of Miss Fry's pupils from the "Along Came a Spider" dance of that year's Frylics show.

April 25: Frylics of '36.

June 11: Some of "Elinor Fry's Stars" perform in *Shrine Jollies of '36* at the Mosque.

December 11: Miss Fry's pupils dance at the John Marshall Hotel for the Local Saints and Sinners Club of America as is accepts toys for needy children.

1937 January 2: Miss Fry gives a dance for Miss Barbara Grundy at the John Marshall Hotel.

February 25: Miss Fry's pupils dance at the Jefferson Hotel for a fashion show and card party hosted by the Patrick Henry School PTA.

March 18: Miss Fry's pupils dance at the John Marshall Hotel for the UDC, Lee Chapter.

May 1: Frylics of '37. Rehearsals were held at the Elks Club.

May 20: Miss Fry's pupils dance at the Chester School to raise money for the school's piano fund.

May 26: Miss Fry's pupils dance at a garden party at the private residence of Lucille Puette for the Randolph-Macon Alumnae Association.

October 28: Miss Fry's pupils dance in a floor show and give a demonstration of the "Big Apple" at a Halloween show at Tantilla Garden.

December 15: Miss Fry's pupils dance the minuet in colonial costume at the Jefferson Hotel for the Daughters of the American Revolution.

1938   April 23: Frylics of '38.

April 27: Dance Revue of Miss Fry's School of Dance at Ladies at Miller & Rhoads Tearoom.

May 19: Miss Fry's pupils dance at the Mosque for Richmond Safety Council.

June 6: Miss Fry's pupils dance at Chester Women's Club.

June 17: Miss Fry's pupils dance at the Mosque for the Bowl of Rice Revue, to help war's innocent victims of China.

September 16: Miss Fry's pupils model clothes for the Juvenile Fashion Show at Miller & Rhoads.

1939   April 29: Frylics of '39.

May 25: Miss Fry's pupils dance at the Mosque for the Industrial Employees and Commercial Vehicle Drivers.

July 30: Miss Fry and her mother visit the Chamberlin-Vanderbilt Hotel at Old Point Comfort.

August 28: Miss Fry's pupils dance at the Jefferson Hotel for the Virginia American Legion Auxiliary.

September 12: Miss Fry and some of her pupils dance at a "Pops" concert at City Stadium for the Richmond Philharmonic Orchestra.

November 25: Miss Fry gives a "Barn Dance" at the William Byrd Hotel in honor of the pupils of her Cotillion.

November 28: Miss Fry's pupils dance at the Thanksgiving Ball at Masonic Temple.

1940 March 5: Ballet by Miss Fry's pupils this week in the Tearoom at Miller & Rhoads for the Children's Book Fair.

April 6: Miss Fry dances and has a meeting at the John Marshall Hotel for the mothers of her pupils.

May 11: Frylics of '40.

June 18: Miss Fry spends two weeks at Cascades Inn in Healing Springs.

October 21: Miss Fry's pupils dance at the Iron Lung Ball at Tantilla Garden.

October 26: The opening dance of Miss Fry's Cotillion Club is held at the William Byrd Hotel.

October 30: Miss Fry's pupils dance the Annual Halloween Dance at Tantilla Garden.

December 22: Miss Fry's pupils dance at the Springhill Avenue home of Miss Emma Lee Costello.

1941 February 11–12: Miss Fry's pupils dance in a musical comedy, *Rio Rita*, at Thomas Jefferson High School to benefit the Catholic Theatre Guild.

February 13: Miss Fry's pupils dance at the John Marshall Hotel for the Retail Coal Merchants Association.

February 20: Miss Fry's pupils dance at the Sphinx Club of Acca Temple Shrine at Ewart's Cafeteria.

April 6: Miss Fry's pupils dance in the Catholic Theatre Guild's *When Pilate Judges* at Thomas Jefferson High School.

April 12: Miss Fry entertains her pupils at the Roof Garden of the John Marshall Hotel.

May 17: Frylics of '41.

September 6: Miss Fry marries Stuart Wesley Phillips.

1942 April 10: Miss Fry's pupils dance at the Women's Club for the Monarch Club of Richmond to buy X-Ray equipment for Sheltering Arms Hospital.

May 16: Frylics of '42—to benefit the Army Emergency Relief Fund and the Elks Charity Fund.

June 25: Miss Fry's pupils dance at John Marshall Hotel for the Richmond League for the Hard of Hearing.

September 29: Miss Fry's pupils dance in the "Okay America Revue" at the Mosque.

November 18: Miss Fry's pupils dance in the annual Thanksgiving Party at the Home for the Incurables.

December 7: Miss Fry's pupils dance for the Catholic Women's Club.

1943 January 23: Miss Fry's pupils dance in the G-3 Revue in the Servicemen's Theatre in the Lyric Theatre.

February 27: Miss Fry's pupils dance in the "The Little Revue" in the Servicemen's Theatre in the Lyric Theatre.

1944 November 2: Miss Fry's pupils dance in the Manchester Lions Club "Roaring Revue."

1945 June 15: Ella Binford, Miss Fry's first dance teacher, dies.

October 13: Miss Fry's pupils dance at the Jefferson Hotel for the Junior German Club.

October 26: Miss Fry's pupils dance at the Robert E. Lee PTA Halloween costume party.

1946 April 1: Miss Fry's pupils dance at the John Marshall for Church Hill Chapter, "That Old Gang of Mine."

November 8: Miss Fry's pupils dance in the Manchester Lions Club "Roaring Revue."

1947 May 17: Frylics of '47.

November 7, 8, 14 and 15: Miss Fry's pupils dance for the eleventh annual Manchester Lions Club "Roaring Revue."

1948 January 18: Several of Miss Fry's pupils dance at the WRVA Theatre in *March of Stars* to benefit the March of Dimes.

May 8: Frylics of '48, *Heaven and Earth*.

1949 January 30: Miss Fry's pupils dance at an WRVA benefit show for the March of Dimes.

March 26: Miss Fry and seventy of her pupils appear in a newsreel at a local theater, taken under the auspices of the Virginia State Chamber of Commerce.

May 21: Frylics of '49, *Present, Past and Future*.

1950 May 6: Frylics of '50, *Frylics of Fifty*.

October 20: Miss Fry's pupils dance at Nathaniel Bacon PTA variety show.

1951   May 5: Frylics of '51, *Our United States.*

May 13: Miss Fry's pupils dance at McGuires's Hospital.

1952   January 21: Miss Fry's pupils dance for the Gay Nineties Party of the Virginia Press Association at the John Marshall Hotel Roof Garden.

January 21: The Annual March of Dimes Giant Benefit Show includes pupils from Miss Fry's School of Dance—"See a Good Show—Fight Polio" at WRVA Theatre.

May 3: Frylics of '52, *Dancing Through Life.*

1953   January 16: Miss Fry's pupils dance at the Third Annual Confederate Ball at the Jefferson Hotel.

May 3: Frylics of '53, *Say It with Flowers.*

1954   May 8: Frylics of '54, *On with the Dance.*

1955   May 7: Frylics of '55, *Hit Parade.*

1956   May: Frylics of '56, *Leisure and Pleasure.*

1957   February 6: Miss Fry's mother (Irene Virginia Hancock Fry) dies.

May 4: Frylics of '57, *Songs of the Islands.*

October 21: Miss Fry and Stuart Phillips are invited to a white tie dinner at the Waldorf-Astoria in honor of Her Majesty Queen Elizabeth II, hosted by the Pilgrims and English Speaking Union.

November 24: Miss Fry's pupils dance for the Special Services, Quartermaster Training Command, Fort Lee.

1958   May 3: Frylics of '58, *Melody of the Bells.*

1959   April 25: Frylics of '59, *A Book Revue of Virginia.*

1960   May: Frylics of '60, *Greetings and Best Wishes.*

1961   March 19: Miss Fry's friend Mabel Puterbaugh dies and is buried in Kansas.

April 29: Frylics of '61, *25th Anniversary Recital.*

1962   May 5: Frylics of '62, *Out of This World.*

1963   May 4: Frylics of '63, *Collector's Items.*

May 19: Miss Fry's pupils dance for the Special Services, Quartermaster Training Command, Fort Lee.

1964   May 2: Frylics of '64, *The Fairest of the Fair.*

1965   May 8: Frylics of '65, *Out of the Magazine Rack.*

1966   May 7: Frylics of '66, *Music the Whole World Loves.*

1967   May 6: Frylics of '67, *Good News.*

1968   May 4: Frylics of '68, *Happiness Is.*

1969   May 3: Frylics of '69, *Love Makes the World Go Round.*

1970   April: Miss Fry is honored with St. Catherine's Distinguished Alumni Award.

   May 9: Frylics of '70, *Moments to Remember.*

   September 24: Richmond Home for Boys puts on a *Vaudeville Is Back* show at the Jefferson Hotel.

1981   April 16: Stuart Wesley Phillips passes away.

1984   January 8: Elinor Fry passes away.

1997   April 19: Virginia Fry Terrell passes away.

NOTES

RNL: *Richmond News Leader.*
RTD: *Richmond Times-Dispatch*
"Scrapbook": items in Miss Fry's scrapbook, retained by Bettie Terrell Dorsey Hobson.
UI: a scrapbook article that had been clipped out of a newspaper or a magazine that did not contain all or some of the following: the author, date and/or name of the publication. Since the scrapbooks are organized by date, it is often possible to discern the year or the decade that an article appeared but not the exact date or the name of the publication. Sometimes the articles showed the author's name but not the date or the name of the publication. Unless otherwise noted, the comments and quotations from former students were made to the author either orally or in writing and are not footnoted. The only quotations from former students that are footnoted are those that were not made to the author.

1. "The man who taught America to sing": UI, scrapbook.
2. Information about Patsy Garrett: *RTD*, March 5, 1950, September 13, 1953, October 14, 1943; and telephone conversation with author; La Verne Lupton: *RTD,* July 7, 1939; March 26, 1940; Edith Wray: *RTD*, May 9, 1942; Mark Ward: *RTD*, December 27, 1953, article by Helen Herrink Fix; also www.playbillvault.com; Eileen Lawlor: 1967 Frylics program; *RTD*, January 21, 1968; Sandra Walker: *RNL*, December 5, 1987; Ruth

Notes

Ann King: 1967 Frylics program; Ellen Robertson, obituary, *RTD*, May 2008; Lynda Beran: *Capital Times* [Madison, WI]; Deborah Smith: *RTD*, November 8, 1968; John Hurdle: *RTD*, November 2, 1969; Patricia Goldman, Pamela Privette Meltzer and Roger Riggle Jr.: conversation(s) with author; Jacqueline Goldberg Jones: conversation with author; www.jacquelinejones.net; Romy Nordlinger: www.romynordlinger.com.

3. "The charming event of the week": *RTD* July 31, 1910; "Simply brought down the house": *RTD*, April 29, 1916; "Pelt[ing] each other...sorts of unique favors": *RTD*, April 29, 1916.

4. "One of the biggest amateur affairs": *RTD*, April 13, 1919.

5. "Exquisite grace as a toe dancer:" G. Watson James, Jr., UI, scrapbook; *Halifax Gazette* [South Boston, VA], June 7, 1927. "With artistic success [her] grace and exquisite dancing": UI, scrapbook.

6. "One of the most beautiful things in the entire performance...was much applauded": *RTD*, November 20, 1921.

7. Contestants—forty-four young women and eleven matrons: *RTD*, August 17, 1921.

8. "Sixteen of Richmond's most attractive girls will dance with all the abandon": *RTD*, December 24, 1922.

9. "Again delighted Richmond audiences": *RTD*, June 1, 1923; "Charming toe solo": *RTD*, May 13, 1923; "One of the most gifted toe-dancers": *Danville* [VA] *Bee*, May 7, 1924.

10. "Widely known as one of the most gifted dancers in Richmond": *RTD*, April 1, 1923; "The delightful Miss Elinor Fry": *RTD*, April 1, 1923.

11. "The big olla-podrida of entertainment": *RTD*, May 2, 1924.

12. "There is a Nature Room...business woman of the first order": *RTD*, October 28, 1923.

13. "Versatility in tap, military tap...and Indian folk dance": *RTD*, April 29, 1951.

14. "Miss Fry's Dancing Dollies": *RTD*, December 10, 1924.

15. Performances at Mosque in February 1931 and November 1932: *RTD*, February 22, 1931; November 6, 1932.

16. Newspaper photo with bathing suit: *RTD*, June 12, 1938; Obituary of Ray Francis: *RTD*, UI, scrapbook.

17. Miss Fry to open studio at 2805 Monument after her return: *RTD*, September 14, 1924.

18. Dances at Mosque for 1950 Tobaccorama: *RTD*, October 8, 1950.

19. Information about Idear Steele Traylor: Louise Ellyson; *RTD*, October 13, 1969; October 4, 1937.

20. "It would break my heart...somewhere else": scrapbook, August 7, 1954.
21. "A new version of the Negro style dancing": *Daily Sketch*, August 1, 1934.
22. Anne Hunter danced a "striking and intricate number": UI, scrapbook.
23. "Their gay good humor will make everyone wish to stay in their hostelry": *RTD*, UI, 1935.
24. Telegram dated May 5, 1957: scrapbook.
25. "Eyes of jewels that glisten...of an older day": *RTD*, May 18, 1935.
26. Pageant of Nations program: scrapbook.
27. Miss Fry and Mabel Puterbaugh were guests at a buffet and swimming pool party: *Hutchinson* [KS] *News*, April 4, 1933; "Somewhat deserted the ranks of society...solo dancing": *Los Angeles Evening Herald and Express*, August 8, 1933; in town for a wedding and then a trip to Denver: *Hutchinson News*, July 1, 1941; Puterbaugh—oldest nonmember attendant: Dance Congress publication, scrapbook.
28. Portrait of Miss Fry by Carl Clarke: *RTD*, February 22, 1925.
29. Moving to 317 West Grace after return from New York: *RTD*, September 8, 1925.
30. "Well known for her grace and artistry and admired beyond Richmond": *RTD*, June 8, 1927.
31. "An ultramodern stage picture": UI, scrapbook.
32. "Sturdy teacher of capers": Dance Congress publication, scrapbook.
33. "A stern curriculum for anyone over 16": *New York World Telegram*, August 10, 1948.
34. "A delightful group of 100...privilege to witness": Dance Congress publication, scrapbook.
35. "Typical of what we think...unobtrusive at all times": Dance Congress publication, scrapbook.
36. "Ring a bell with any serviceman": *RTD*, July 23, 1955.
37. "Parents wished bon voyage...the trip too": *RTD*, July 23, 1955.
38. Information about the Mosque: original 1927 Mosque program, scrapbook; "Lithe and graceful children": *RTD*, December 30, 1927; "Run by the people for the people": *RTD*, December 30, 1927; "Regarded as one of Richmond's ablest dancers": *RTD*, December 30, 1927.
39. "Wear and tear on the teachers...and oh, you name it": *RTD*, March 30, 1958.
40. Insurance information: invoices in scrapbook.
41. Dress rehearsal instructions: scrapbook.
42. "From the severe military coats...swan costumes": UI, scrapbook.
43. "A mother whose child is really to be a blackbird...buttons for eyes": Edith Lindeman, *RTD*, April 17, 1955.

44. "Within a few weeks...eagle eye of each mother": UI, scrapbook.
45. "An effort is made to keep...during the winter": Edith Lindeman, *RTD*, July 23, 1955.
46. "Decked out as cowboys...even the married ones come back": *RTD*, April 17, 1955.
47. "Dressed in raggle taggle...a real show stopper": Diane Hile, *RNL*, July 21, 1965.
48. Rental of studio was seventy-five dollars per month in 1964: invoice in scrapbook.
49. Parking lot canteen: *RTD*, July 22, 1943; Stoopnagle: *RTD*, September 12, 1943.
50. "Skinny Ennis in reverse": *RTD*, June 7, 1943.
51. Advertisement for a pianist: *RTD*, September 23, 1945.
52. "Internationally Known Blind Woman Will Demonstrate Her Remarkable Genius": *RTD*, May 20, 1933; Emma Livingston, *RTD*, July 6, 1970.
53. "Unquenchable spirit...teaching ability:" Edith Lindeman, *RTD*, May 18, 1942.
54. "I can't—me tail's taught": Anne Ball, *RNL*, April 15, 1970.
55. "All the time fighting gallantly...laughed at my own children": Anne Ball, *RNL*, April 15, 1970.
56. "In Arab uniforms and wearing the fez": *RTD*, June 9, 1927.
57. "Sweet Ingénue...Especially charming...with spirit and finish": *RTD*, April 30, 1927.
58. Article about Richmond women working outside the home: *RTD*, June 8, 1927.
59. "Intently observed as the history...the Mardi Gras spirit": UI, scrapbook.
60. "A dance and whoopee": *RTD*, April 24, 1929.
61. "Hear and See Movietone news...little dancing girls": *RTD*, February 12, 1929.
62. "A real girlie-girlie show": *New Orleans Times-Picayune*, July 14, 1929.
63. "A bewitching dance specialty": *RTD*, December 29, 1926.
64. "Phantasmagoria of bizarre sights and sounds": *RTD*, December 8, 1925.
65. Bowl of Rice Revue: *RTD*, June 18, 1938.
66. "As thoroughly graceful and delightful...tremendous applause": *RTD*, February 20, 1929.
67. Advertisement for Miss Fry's dog Buster: *RTD*, December 13, 1914; drawings by local kids: *RTD*, February 4, 1917.
68. "A brilliant function...of pink roses": *RTD*, December 23, 1922.

69. Attended *Tangerine* with Clarence Boykin: *RTD*, October 31, 1922.

70. *Los Angeles Herald and Express*, August 8, 1933.

71. "Miss Elinor Fry's Skating Lassies": advertisement in *RTD* for Cavalier Arena, June 21, 25, 26, 27, 1942.

72. "Pseudo-televised visit to the land of gypsies": UI, by Ann Faulkner.

73. "Kindergarten polka": *RTD*, April 2, 1910.

74. "Happiness is" note from Miss Fry to her students: scrapbook.

75. Thank-you note from Washington and Lee University: scrapbook.

76. "Story of tobacco in song and dance": *RTD*, October 11, 1949.

77. "A need and request for fresh, young faces and spirited pretty dancing": *RTD*, April 17, 1955.

78. A crowd of 4,700 at the mosque: *RTD*, May 14, 1942.

79. "After fifteen minutes of almost unbelievable immobility": *RTD*, May 18, 1942, Edith Lindeman.

80. "January was ushered in...flowers of autumn": *RTD*, May 18, 1942, Edith Lindeman.

81. "Little girls in lavender...three inches": UI, scrapbook.

82. "An exquisite ballet...Richmond audiences": Edith Lindeman, *RTD*, April 30, 1939.

83. "The same swift...with this group." Edith Lindeman, *RTD*, 1940 (specific date unidentified).

84. "Add[ed] new laurels...laud it to the skies": *RTD*, 1934 (specific date unidentified).

85. "Well-planned...in color and design": Helen de Motte, *RTD*, 1934 (specific date unidentified).

86. "Moonlight and Roses...the former Elinor Fry": *RTD*, February 8, 1942.

87. Retiring in part because of her husband's health: Anne Ball, *RNL*, April 15, 1970.

88. "Retains the dancer's quality...are limitless": Anne Ball, *RNL*, April 15, 1970.

89. "When I received the notice from St. Catherine's...so many 'Moments to Remember'": St. Catherine's Archives.

90. "The most intriguing...thank you": scrapbook.

91. Margaret Woodburn quote: letter to the editor, UI, scrapbook.

92. Grayson Jones quote: letter to the editor, UI, scrapbook.

93. "The joy of learning...a wonderful day": scrapbook, author unknown.

94. "In the past few weeks...thou art": Robert Watkins, scrapbook. Courtesy of Robert Watkins and de Veaux Riddick.

95. La Sylphide poem by Patsy Bickerstaff: courtesy of Patsy Bickerstaff.

96. "It makes me very sad...the thrill": *RNL*, April 15, 1970.
97. Helen Coleman quote: letter to the editor, UI, scrapbook.
98. "Your life lies before you...": scrapbook.

SOURCES

Daily Sketch, August 1, 1934.

Los Angeles Evening Herald and Express, August 8, 1933.

New Orleans Times –Picayune, July 14, 1929.

Rappahannock Times, June 22, 1944.

Richmond News Leader, 1965, 1970, 1987.

Richmond Times Dispatch, various issues, 1906–1970.

INDEX

A

Adams, Ed 89
Ahern, Cheryl (Weis) 40, 58, 73
Ahern, Jo Ann 98
Archbell, Nancy Lee (Bain) 14, 77, 78, 94
Atkinson, Mary Clay 78

B

Bacigalupo, Edythe 52, 56
Bacigalupo, Lina Lee (Butler) 40, 59, 60, 107
Bagby, Darlene 78
Bambacus, Larry 98
Barker, Nancy (Jones) 56, 89, 90
Barron, Jean 40
Beaux Arts Ball 44, 110, 124
Beckh sisters 95
Beran, Lynda 19
Bickerstaff, Bill 100
Bickerstaff, Doris 45, 51, 53, 54
Bickerstaff, Patsy 45, 51, 59, 110, 113
Binford, Ella 23, 24, 33, 105, 115, 116, 128
Binford, Katherine 24
Bloxsom, Bette (Witherington) 14, 32, 51, 54, 56, 75, 92

Bloxsom, Grace (Cofer) 12, 97
Bowman, Dale Adams 56
Boyer, Anne 24, 26, 33, 96, 105
Boykin, Clarence 68, 117
Bradley, Betty (Jones) 56, 78
Branner, Adair Lee 75
Branner, Marjorie (Adams) 36
Branner, Suzanne (Kessler) 18, 51
Brewer, Angela 62
Broom, Kevin Stewart 78
Brown, Hill 51
Bryan, Henry 56
Bryant, Hertha 17, 121

C

Cabell, James Branch 23, 65, 105, 116
Cadmus, Shirley 44, 122
Cannon, Anne 91
Cavalier Arena 69, 75
Chapman, Ruby 24
Cilimberg, Alma 58
Coleman, Helen 113
Connell, Cornelia 19, 56, 87
Crowder, Barbara Elizabeth (Jensen) 14
Crowder, Laura 101
Curley, George 62

D

David twins 95
Davis, Berkeley 24, 105
Denishawn Dance Studio 43
Donnan, Cleiland 24
Dorsey, Terry (Dalton) 76, 108
Duncan, Isadora 65, 123

E

Ed Sullivan Show, The 46
Edwards, Nancy Lynn (Siford) 14, 54, 62
Elcorise School of Dancing 34

F

Farley, Dorothy (Bennett) 56, 78, 94
Finke, Alyce Ann 36
Fiske, Linda (Wehrle) 73
Ford, Skippy 78
Frances, Kay 18
Francis, Ray 30
Fry, Irene Virginia 21, 22, 129
Fry, Pamela 98
Fry, Peter 9, 21, 22, 115
Fry, Peter, Jr. 22, 43, 115, 124
Fry, Virginia 22, 115, 116, 117, 130

G

Galloway, Anne 46, 80
Galloway, James 46, 47, 51, 98
Garrett, Mickey 56, 77
Garrett, Patsy 16, 17, 27, 40, 51, 59,
    60, 61, 64, 75, 78, 89, 91, 113
Goldberg, Jacqueline (Jones) 21, 40, 113
Goldberg Sisters 83
Goldman, Patricia Lee 14, 20
Griffith, Mary 87, 119
Grundy, Barbara 28, 125

H

Hanes, Sam 64
Harper, Julia Mildred 24, 33, 34
Hasty, W.D., Jr. 78

Hazelgrove, Bill 107
Henley, Gilbert 40, 79
Herbert, Seldon 66
Herguner, Sarah 105
Heritage School of the Dance 34
Hobson, Bettie Terrell Dorsey 9, 10,
    21, 22, 60, 69, 78, 89, 90, 108
Hobson, Page (Bourgeois) 71
Hooker, Virginia Lee 25
Hope, Bob 56
Horton, Gentry 36
Hunter, Anne 36, 60
Hurdle, John 19
Hutzler, Gale (Hargroves) 14, 39, 58, 78

J

Jefferson Hotel 21, 22, 23, 25, 44, 55,
    64, 65, 68, 69, 79, 87, 107, 110,
    115, 116, 117, 120, 124, 125,
    126, 128, 129, 130
John Marshall Hotel 50, 55, 65, 66, 69,
    87, 123, 124, 125, 127, 128, 129
Jolson, Al 60
Jones, Grayson 108

K

Kaminsky, Jack 34, 56
Keller, Helen 59, 106
Kent, Harriette 15, 64
Kessler, John 56
King, Ruth Ann 19, 80

L

Landmark Theatre 10, 48
Lange sisters 78, 94
Lawlor, Eileen 19, 75
Lewis sisters 36, 78, 95
Lindeman, Edith 48, 51, 52, 54, 59,
    72, 92, 94, 101, 102
Lisman, Gerald 55
Long, Fay (Lovering) 89, 90
Lupton, La Verne 18, 78

M

MacLaine, Shirley 21
Markel, Debra Margaret 35, 40
Markel, Zelda 35
Marker, Linda 101
Marks, Helen 56
Markward, Edward 19
Massei, Anna 29, 34
McKee, Cecelia (Marano) 34, 54
McKemmie, Billie 77, 78
Mease, Marion (Childrey) 19, 33, 34,
    44, 56, 58, 60, 72, 75, 89, 94, 95
Miller & Rhoads 55, 126, 127
Mills, Warren 64
Mosque 10, 17, 25, 29, 32, 33, 34, 38,
    41, 48, 50, 55, 60, 65, 66, 67,
    68, 79, 87, 99, 110, 120, 121,
    122, 123, 124, 125, 126, 128

N

National Geographic 86, 87, 121
Neal, Paula 101
Nordlinger, Romy 21, 113
Norman, Carol 95

O

Ogg, Nancy (Tripp) 14, 35, 104
Ogg, Virginia 35
Ogg, Wade 14, 54, 79

P

Parker, Joanna Forrest 101
Phillips, Stuart Wesley 19, 45, 103,
    104, 106, 115, 127, 129, 130
Poe, Edgar Allan 99
Powder Puff Girls 27
Powell, Helen O. 56, 61
Pratt, Claudia Wilson 13, 47, 60
Privette, Jana (Usry) 16, 78, 83
Privette, Pamela (Meltzer) 14, 58, 83
Privette, Pamela (Usry) 20
Privette, Renee 83
Puterbaugh, Mabel 42, 43, 129

R

Reynolds, Anne 68, 77
Riddick, de Veaux 62, 135
Riggle, Amy 97
Riggle, Roger, Jr. 21, 72, 77, 97, 104,
    113
Rippe, Hazel 78
Robinson, Bill "Bojangles" 27

S

Salsbury, Harriet 73
Salsbury, Linda (Weinstein) 12, 20, 28,
    46, 80, 100, 113
San Carlo Opera Company 17, 18
Schneider, David Allan 76
Schwab, Ellis 36, 92
Seal, Carolyn 34, 56, 58
Seldon, Gwendolyn 23, 116
Sharp, Cindy K. 56, 78
Shenfield, Anna 56
Slater, Winifred (Hazelton) 13, 31, 40,
    71
Smith, Deborah 19, 68
Smith, Joey 64, 98
Sneed, Schuyler 14
Soden, Frank 56
St. Catherine's School 30, 31, 105,
    106, 107
Stewart, Susan (Porter) 12
Stoddart, Lucille 33, 44, 45

T

Tantilla Garden 18, 30, 32, 66, 125,
    126, 127
Temple, Shirley 55, 69, 75, 97
Terrell, Bettie (Dorsey Hobson).
    See Hobson, Bettie Terrell
    Dorsey
Thalhimer's 55, 123
Thomas, Jane 56, 79
Thompson, Emily 17, 87, 118, 119
Todd, Mary 18, 43, 87, 119, 120
Tray-Boy 24, 25, 33, 34, 41, 96, 105,
    117, 124

Traylor, Constance (Ackerman) 12, 34
Traylor, Idear Steele 24, 25, 26, 33, 34,
    35, 65, 96, 105
Troxell, Charlotte 56
Troxell, Mark 56
Tyler, Donna Ellen 36
Tyler, Jane Ellen 100

V

Viener, Jacqueline 35

W

Walker, Sandra 19
Waring, Fred 16
Watkins, Helen Lindsey 58
Watkins, Robert 109
Weaver, Jody (Yuhass) 75, 92
Wells, Corlease 24
Wolfe, Tom 17
Woodburn, Margaret 34, 56, 108
Wray, Edith 18, 41
Wright, Raymond 78
Wyland, Anita 17, 87, 119, 121

Y

Yonan, Becky 14

ABOUT THE AUTHOR

Paul N. Herbert is the author of *The Jefferson Hotel: The History of a Richmond Landmark* and *God Knows All Your Names*, a collection of short, true stories of obscure and lesser-known events in American history (despite the title, the book is not about religion). Paul and his wife, Pam, and their two sons, Alex and Bill, live in northern Virginia. He can be reached at elinorfrybook@ yahoo.com.

Visit us at
www.historypress.net
....

This title is also available as an e-book